CLAIM YOUR SUCCESS

THE ULTIMATE GUIDE TO STARTING AND RUNNING A PUBLIC INSURANCE ADJUSTING BUSINESS

CHIP MERLIN

LYNETTE YOUNG

CLAIM YOUR SUCCESS LLC

CONTENTS

ISBN-13: 979-8-9913216-0-0 (Ebook Edition)

ISBN-13: 979-8-9913216-1-7 (Hardcover Edition)

Cover by Ben Donnell, Donnell Creative LLC

Edited by Kate Hannisian, Blue Pencil Consulting

www.ClaimYourSuccessBook.com

To all those that help policyholders.

FOREWARD - JUSTIN SKIPTON

As a seasoned public adjuster with nearly two decades of experience, I have dedicated my career to advocating for policyholders and advancing our profession. My involvement with the National Association of Public Insurance Adjusters (NAPIA) has been central to that mission, and I am honored to currently serve in the officer line, slated to become the 2025–2026 President during NAPIA's 75th year. This journey has been guided by a simple but powerful philosophy: to be the best at what you do, you must always seek to learn and improve.

Claim Your Success: The Ultimate Guide to Starting and Running a Public Insurance Adjusting Business embodies that philosophy. While it serves as a foundational guide for new public adjusters, its insights extend far beyond the basics. This book is a resource for anyone — seasoned adjusters included — seeking to refine their craft, enhance their business, or better serve their clients.

The authors, Chip Merlin and Lynette Young, are uniquely positioned to share these lessons. Early in my career, I had the privilege of meeting both Chip and Lynette, and their influence on my professional growth has been immeasurable. Chip, one of the leading plaintiff bad faith attorneys in the industry, has dedicated his life to educating public adjusters, creating forums that empower us to excel. Lynette, a pioneer in public adjusting software, has revolutionized the tools we use while gaining unparalleled insight into what makes public adjusters succeed — or fail.

This book reflects their deep understanding of the challenges and opportunities in our profession. Whether you are just beginning your journey or have years of experience, it offers actionable strategies, practical tools, and a roadmap to success in an ever-evolving industry.

As you read these pages, I encourage you to embrace the mindset of continuous improvement and learning. The knowledge within is not just about building a business; it's about building a legacy of excellence, integrity, and advocacy.

Sincerely,

Justin R. Skipton, AIC, SPPA

Skipton Claims Management

FOREWARD - WILLIAM MIDTBO

After working for Chip Merlin for close to a decade, I have since opened the doors to my own public adjusting firm. Chip's mentorship was invaluable and a cornerstone of my professional growth. He stands at the pinnacle of first-party property law, with accolades to prove it. I had the privilege of learning from one of the best and most ethical mentors in the field. His constant reminders echo in my mind: "Do the right thing, don't cut corners, stay out of trouble, follow the rules, and don't mess this up."

In this business, I've seen many come and go, but Chip's unwavering emphasis on ethical practices for public adjusters has stayed with me. He's more than an insurance expert — he's an empathetic advocate for policyholders facing some of the toughest moments in their lives. Whether traveling the country to give educational speeches or engaging with public adjusters, he embodies passion and integrity. If you ever see him speak, be prepared: he has a knack for playfully calling you out in front of the crowd or even answering your phone if it rings during his talk.

I also had the opportunity to work closely with Lynette for

many years. Her bubbly personality, paired with her deep expertise in assisting public adjusters with CRNs and processes, is unmatched. Lynette goes out of her way to answer questions and customize solutions to meet the unique needs of public adjusters. Her extensive knowledge of public adjusting is a resource I continually draw upon.

My time with both Chip and Lynette has been like a masterclass in public adjusting that I didn't even realize I was attending at the time. The connections I've built with experts and fellow public adjusters during this period have proven invaluable. Although I've heard much of the content in this book multiple times, I still find myself learning something new every day. Being a public adjuster requires proficiency in numerous areas, and there's no single book or class that can teach it all. Take it one day at a time, seek out multiple mentors as I did, and you'll find the sky is the limit.

If I could offer one key piece of advice for growing your firm, it's this: always answer your phone. Building trust and maintaining open communication will lead to opportunities and claims following naturally. Best of luck on your journey.

Sincerely,
William Midtbo
Prime Adjustments

INTRODUCTION

THE SIGNIFICANCE OF PUBLIC INSURANCE ADJUSTING

Let's dive into an exciting and fulfilling journey: becoming a public adjuster. This isn't just about landing a job; it's an opportunity to create your own business, become your own boss, and make a meaningful impact in people's lives at their most challenging times.

Imagine being the hero for someone who's overwhelmed by property damage. As a public adjuster, you represent these individuals, ensuring their insurance claims are handled fairly and justly. This role is a unique blend of empathy, expertise, and negotiation skills. You'll need to master understanding insurance policies, meticulously assessing damages, and confidently negotiating with insurance companies. It's all about finding that sweet spot where compassion meets assertiveness.

Developing expertise in damage assessment is crucial. You'll learn to identify the subtle damages and accurately estimate repair costs, ensuring your clients get the compensation they deserve. This skill sets you apart, allowing you to see what others might miss.

Chances are if you have picked up this book, you might have an inkling of what a public adjuster is and what they do. What you may not know is all the ways to start and run a public adjusting *business*.

Now, turning this role into a successful business is where the real adventure begins. The first-party claims industry, despite any inefficiencies, offers a wealth of opportunities for entrepreneurs like you. These aren't just challenges; they're your stepping stones to success. Your business can address the delays, underpayments, and inadequate service that plague the property insurance industry.

The first step on your journey to becoming a successful public adjuster is education and certification. Understanding the legal requirements in your area is essential, as each state may have specific rules and regulations governing this profession. Typically, this involves completing specific courses and obtaining certifications.

To get started, you'll need to enroll in a reputable training program that covers the fundamentals of public insurance adjusting. These programs often include courses on insurance law, policy language, damage assessment, negotiation techniques, and ethical considerations. It's essential to choose a program that offers a well-rounded education and practical experience.

Once you've completed the required coursework, you'll need to pass a state certification exam and secure a bond to become a licensed public adjuster. This exam assesses your knowledge of insurance policies, claims handling procedures, and the legal aspects of the profession. Passing the exam is a significant milestone on your path to becoming a successful adjuster, but it is not the only tool you need for success.

With your education and certification in hand, it's time to develop a solid business plan. Your business plan will serve as your road map to success, guiding you through the steps needed to establish and grow your public insurance adjusting business.

Becoming a public adjuster and establishing your own

business is a rewarding journey filled with opportunities for personal and professional growth. From education and certification to networking and marketing, each step plays a crucial role in building a successful public adjusting business.

Remember that your role goes beyond business; you are a trusted advocate for individuals and businesses facing property damage. Your expertise and dedication can make a significant difference in their lives, and in return, you'll find financial success and personal fulfillment in this challenging and rewarding profession.

Embrace the adventure, stay committed to continuous learning, and prioritize your clients, and you'll find that being a public adjuster is not just a career choice; *it's a calling.*

Note

It isn't typical for a brand-new public adjuster to start a business unless you have some sort of experience in the greater restoration industry. Typical paths to public adjusting and business ownership come from carrier adjusting, roofing sales, restoration, general contracting, or even working inside another public adjusting company.

It's crucial to note that even seasoned, multi-generational public adjusting companies stand to gain tremendously from this book. The insights it offers are not just foundational but deeply enriching, capable of introducing even the most experienced professionals to new strategies and perspectives. This depth of knowledge benefits all levels of expertise, from the novice stepping into the industry with a robust background in related fields, to legacy firms looking to modernize practices and expand their understanding of current consumer needs and legal frameworks. This book acts as a bridge, connecting varied experiences with the specialized world of public adjusting, ensuring every reader comes away better equipped to thrive in this dynamic field.

WHY CHIP AND LYNETTE?

Chip Merlin and Lynette Young bring a wealth of experience, insight, and unmatched expertise to the public adjusting industry. Despite not being public adjusters themselves, they are the perfect duo to author a book on business-building in this field. Their unique backgrounds make them ideally suited to guide both newcomers and seasoned professionals.

Chip and Lynette provide a comprehensive view of the public adjusting industry. *Claim Your Success* covers all the essentials you need to know to successfully operate a public adjusting firm. The book is a valuable business resource, offering complete coverage of topics relevant to public adjusters. The book is based on a lifetime of experiences, from setting up public adjusters to run their own businesses, to business growth strategies tailored for the public adjustment industry, addressing both the external challenges of dealing with insurance companies and the internal challenges of running a successful firm. Chip and Lynette's combined expertise provides a comprehensive toolkit for public adjusters to navigate the complexities of the insurance landscape and build thriving enterprises.

Their authority to write on this subject is reinforced not just by their professional achievements but by their unwavering commitment to public adjuster education, public adjuster trade organizations, and hands-on experience answering virtually every type of question a public adjuster would ask in the operation of their firm. They have dedicated themselves to sharing unique knowledge and experience gained through consulting with over a thousand public adjusting firms across the country. They are sought-after speakers whose engagements are about teaching and encouraging public adjusters in the struggles of their profession. This book is an extension of that mission — a guide compiled by two experts who, although coming from different backgrounds, share a common goal of helping public adjusters excel professionally and financially in their profession.

In essence, Chip and Lynette's combined knowledge, experience, and savvy make them the perfect pair to author this definitive guide on building successful public adjusting businesses. They offer you the tools to succeed and the wisdom to navigate the challenges inherent in the field. This unique combination of legal insight, business strategy, and a deep understanding of the public adjusting profession sets this book apart as an authoritative resource.

WHO IS RICH?

In crafting this comprehensive guide to starting and running a successful public adjusting business, we recognized the need for a relatable narrative that could bring our concepts to life. Enter Rich, our fictional protagonist whose journey through the world of public adjusting serves as a powerful learning tool for readers.

Rich's story is more than just an entertaining subplot; it's a carefully constructed narrative designed to illustrate the key principles, challenges, and triumphs that aspiring and established public adjusters might encounter. Through Rich's experiences, readers can see the practical application of the strategies and advice offered in each chapter.

As you follow Rich's journey from a newcomer in the field to a successful business owner, you'll find that his story mirrors the structure of the book. Each chapter in Rich's tale corresponds to a major topic in the main text, providing a real-world context for the concepts discussed.

We encourage readers to use Rich's story as a reflection point. After reading each chapter, take a moment to consider how Rich applied (or sometimes failed to apply) the principles discussed. Ask yourself:

1. How did Rich's actions align with the chapter's teachings?
2. What challenges did Rich face, and how do they relate to potential obstacles in your own journey?
3. How can you apply the lessons from Rich's experiences to your own public adjusting practice?

By engaging with Rich's story in this way, you'll find that the theoretical becomes practical, the abstract becomes concrete, and the lessons become more memorable and applicable to your own professional growth.

Remember, while Rich is fictional, he was created out of real-world experiences that are rooted in the real-world challenges and opportunities that public adjusters face every day. His story is designed to inspire, educate, and provide a roadmap for your own success in the field of public adjusting.

HOW TO USE THIS BOOK

READ SEQUENTIALLY

While each chapter can stand alone, the book is structured to build your knowledge progressively. Start with the foundational chapters on understanding the insurance industry and legal landscape before moving on to more advanced topics.

FOCUS ON RELEVANT SECTIONS

If you're already established in the field, you may want to focus on specific sections that address your current needs, such as scaling your business or enhancing client relationships.

IMPLEMENT AS YOU LEARN

Don't just read passively. As you encounter new strategies or tools, try to implement them in your practice. This hands-on approach will help solidify your understanding and improve your business.

UTILIZE THE RESOURCES

Take advantage of any checklists or templates provided throughout the book. These tools are designed to help you apply the concepts directly to your business.

REVISIT REGULARLY

As your business grows and evolves, different sections of the book will become more relevant. Keep it as a reference and revisit chapters as needed.

NETWORK AND SHARE

Use the insights gained from this book to engage with other professionals in the field. Share your experiences and learn from others who are on similar journeys.

STAY UPDATED

The insurance industry is constantly changing. Use this book as a foundation, but stay committed to ongoing learning through industry publications, workshops, and continuing education. For the most current information and resources, visit ClaimYourSuccessBook.com. This companion website is regularly updated with:

- The latest business and industry information
- Expanded chapters that dive deeper into key topics
- Downloadable resources, templates, and tools
- By frequently checking the website, you'll ensure you're always working with the most up-to-date information and strategies. This online resource is designed to complement the book and provide

ongoing support as you build and grow your public adjusting business.

REFLECT AND ADAPT

After reading each chapter, take time to reflect on how the information applies to your specific situation. Adapt the strategies to fit your unique business needs and goals.

SEEK ADDITIONAL GUIDANCE

While this book provides comprehensive information, don't hesitate to seek additional guidance from mentors, legal professionals, or business advisors when needed.

Remember, *Claim Your Success* is not just a one-time read, but a guide to accompany you throughout your career in public insurance adjusting. Use it as a road map to navigate the complexities of the industry and build a successful, ethical, and client-focused business.

RICH'S INTRODUCTION

Rich's journey into the world of insurance and public adjusting had its roots in his formative years. As a teenager, Rich spent his summers working for his uncle's construction business, where he gained hands-on experience in building and repair work. These early experiences laid the foundation for his understanding of property structures and the complexities involved in restoration after damage.

After high school, Rich pursued a degree in business administration at college, where he honed his analytical and management skills. Upon graduation, he landed a job as an entry-level desk adjuster at a well-recognized insurance company. Over the years, Rich worked his way up the corporate ladder, earning promotions and gaining valuable experience in claims management.

As time passed, Rich's frustration with the insurance industry's inefficiencies and inadequacies grew. He witnessed countless policyholders struggle to get their claims processed in a timely manner, only to receive inadequate compensation for their losses. The bureaucratic red tape, slow response times, and lack of transparency were all too common. It was as if the industry was failing those it was meant to protect.

Rich's decision to embark on an entrepreneurial journey was not driven by the desire for personal wealth or recognition. It was rooted in a deep-seated belief that policyholders deserved better. He was motivated by the opportunity to create a business that prioritized the needs of the clients above all else. He wanted to build a company that would provide policyholders with the support and advocacy they needed during their most challenging times.

Drawing on his construction background, business education, and years of insurance industry experience, Rich envisioned a public adjusting business that would focus on accuracy in assessing damages, transparency in the claims process, and unwavering dedication to securing fair compensation for policyholders. He saw an opportunity to bridge the gap between policyholders and insurance companies, ensuring that claims were handled fairly and justly.

PART ONE
HISTORY OF INSURANCE AND PUBLIC ADJUSTING

CHAPTER 1
UNDERSTANDING THE INSURANCE INDUSTRY

> It is not the strongest of the species that survive, nor the most intelligent, but the one most responsive to change.
>
> CHARLES DARWIN

UNDERSTANDING the complex landscape of the insurance market isn't just helpful for public adjusters – it's absolutely essential for success in the field. From its origins in maritime trade to today's trillion-dollar marketplace, the insurance industry stands as a cornerstone of the global economy, shaping how businesses and individuals manage risk and protect their assets.

For public adjusters, a deep comprehension of both historical insurance principles and current market operations, including stakeholder roles, regulatory frameworks, and market dynamics, provides the foundation for effectively advocating for policyholders. Without this crucial knowledge, even the most skilled adjuster may find themselves unable to navigate the intricate web of policies, precedents, and procedures that govern insurance claims. As the insurance landscape continuously evolves with new products, changing regulations, and emerging risks, staying informed about market trends and developments becomes vital for maintaining a competitive edge and delivering optimal results for clients.

OVERVIEW OF THE INSURANCE MARKET

The insurance market in the United States is vast and multifaceted, encompassing a wide range of insurance products and services. It includes everything from property and casualty insurance to life and health insurance, serving millions of individuals and businesses.

The industry has witnessed significant growth and has evolved in response to changing market dynamics, technological advancements, and regulatory changes. Trends such as the increasing use of technology in underwriting and claims, the rise of insurtech startups, and changes in consumer behavior all continue to shape the industry.

EARLY BEGINNINGS: THE 18TH CENTURY

The concept of property insurance in the United States took root in the 18th century, influenced heavily by British practices. Following the Great Fire of London in 1666, fire insurance emerged as a necessity. The American colonies, still under British influence, began experimenting with this form of risk management. The Philadelphia Contributionship, founded in 1752 by Benjamin Franklin and others, stands as the first American fire insurance company. Its formation marked a significant step towards organized risk management in the colonies.

EXPANSION AND DIVERSIFICATION: 19TH CENTURY

The 19th century witnessed a significant expansion and diversification of the property insurance industry in the US. The era saw the rise of numerous insurance companies, responding to the growing demand for more comprehensive risk coverage. This period was characterized by the formation of both mutual and stock insurance companies, each catering to different segments of society. The mutual companies, owned by policyholders, focused primarily on rural and small-town markets. In contrast, stock companies, owned by investors, targeted urban centers, and offered a broader range of insurance products.

Regulatory Framework and Standardization

A pivotal aspect of the 19th-century insurance landscape was the establishment of a regulatory framework and standardization of practices. States began enacting laws to regulate insurance companies, aiming to protect policyholders and ensure the solvency of insurers. These regulations covered various aspects, including minimum capital requirements, reserve funds, and the filing of annual reports. This period also saw the development of standardized policy forms and clauses, simplifying and clarifying insurance contracts for both insurers and insureds.

INFLUENCE OF MAJOR DISASTERS

The impact of major urban fires profoundly influenced the property insurance industry. Notable among these were the New York fire of 1835 and the Chicago and Boston fires in the 1870s. These catastrophic events exposed the vulnerabilities in the insurance system, leading to significant changes in underwriting practices, risk assessment, and rate setting. Insurance companies became more cautious in their coverage offerings, with some withdrawing from high-risk areas altogether. These events underscored the need for better risk management strategies and more robust financial reserves.

TECHNOLOGICAL ADVANCES AND INNOVATION

The late 19th and early 20th centuries saw technological advancements that significantly impacted the property insurance industry. The introduction of fire insurance maps, pioneered by the Sanborn Map Company, revolutionized risk assessment practices. These detailed maps provided crucial information on the construction materials, occupancy, and fire protection measures of buildings, allowing insurers to make more informed underwriting decisions.

Growth and Professionalization

As the US economy grew and urbanized, the demand for more sophisticated property insurance products increased. The industry responded with the development of specialized departments within insurance companies, focusing on areas such as fire prevention, engineering inspections, and claims handling. This era marked the professionalization of the industry, with the emergence of industry associations, standardized training programs, and professional designations for insurance practitioners.

GOVERNMENT INVOLVEMENT AND STATE SUPERVISION

Government involvement in the insurance industry intensified during the late 19th and early 20th centuries. State supervision became more pronounced, with the establishment of insurance departments and commissions tasked with overseeing the industry's operations. These regulatory bodies played a crucial role in ensuring the financial stability of insurance companies, protecting consumer interests, and fostering a competitive marketplace.

State insurance regulation in the United States plays a critical role in ensuring the stability, reliability, and integrity of the insurance industry. This regulatory framework is designed to protect policyholders, maintain fair and competitive markets, and foster a healthy insurance ecosystem. Central to this regulatory system is the National Association of Insurance Commissioners (NAIC), an organization that significantly influences insurance regulation across states.

Insurance regulation in the US is primarily the responsibility of individual states, rather than the federal government. Each state has its own insurance department, headed by an insurance commissioner, responsible for overseeing the operations of insurance companies within their jurisdiction. State regulation covers various aspects, including licensing of insurers and agents, approval of policy forms and rates, financial solvency of insurance companies, consumer protection, and market conduct.

The diversity of state regulations, while allowing for localized control and responsiveness to state-specific needs, also poses challenges in terms of consistency and reciprocity among states. This is where the NAIC comes into play. The NAIC, comprising the chief insurance regulators from each of the fifty states, the District of Columbia, and five U.S. territories, serves as a standard-setting and regulatory support organization. It aims to provide a platform for the development of uniform regulatory policies, promoting consistency and cooperation among different state insurance departments.

One of the key contributions of the NAIC is the development of model laws and regulations. These models serve as templates that states can adopt or adapt, fostering greater uniformity in insurance regulation across the country. The NAIC also facilitates information exchange and coordination among state regulators, especially in areas such as financial solvency oversight, market conduct examinations, and consumer protection.

Moreover, the NAIC plays a pivotal role in representing state insurance regulatory interests at the federal level and in international insurance discussions. It ensures the state-based insurance regulatory system is recognized and preserved in national and global policy dialogues.

IMPACT OF LEGISLATION

Legislation played a crucial role in shaping the property insurance industry. Laws such as the McCarran-Ferguson Act of 1945, which affirmed the state regulation of insurance and exempted the industry from certain federal regulations, had a lasting impact. Additionally, the introduction of laws related to unfair claims practices provided a framework for the ethical handling of insurance claims, directly impacting the role and responsibilities of public adjusters. State legislation also allows for the licensing and regulatory oversight of all adjusters, including public adjusters.

MODERN ERA: COMPLEXITY AND CHALLENGES

The latter half of the 20th century and the early 21st century have seen the property insurance industry evolve into a complex and dynamic sector. Challenges such as climate change, natural disasters, and technological risks have necessitated continuous adaptation and innovation. The industry has responded with the development of new insurance products, risk modeling techniques, and a greater emphasis on loss prevention and mitigation.

THE BASICS OF PUBLIC INSURANCE ADJUSTING

At its core, public insurance adjusting is both an art and a science, requiring a delicate balance of technical expertise, negotiation skills, and unwavering advocacy for policyholders. While insurance companies employ their own adjusters to evaluate claims, public adjusters serve as independent professionals who work exclusively for policyholders, ensuring their clients receive fair and maximum compensation for their covered losses.

The Role of Public Insurance Adjusters in Claim Indemnification

Public insurance adjusters are professionals who represent the interests of the policyholder in the insurance claims process. Unlike adjusters who work for insurance companies, public adjusters are hired by policyholders to assess and negotiate insurance claims. Their role is pivotal in ensuring policyholders receive the compensation they are due involving claims with their own insurance companies. They meticulously evaluate property damage, prepare detailed valuations of loss, assist in post-loss obligation compliance, and advocate on behalf of the policyholder during the claim settlement process.

Expertise in Assessing Damages and Valuing Claims

The expertise required by public insurance adjusters is indispensable in accurately assessing property damage according to the full extent of the available policy coverage. They must possess the technical knowledge necessary to interpret insurance policies and identify covered damages accurately. Their skill in correctly valuing claims ensures policyholders receive a fair and just settlement reflecting the true extent of the loss incurred under the available coverage.

Helping Policyholders Navigate the Claims Process

Public insurance adjusters offer numerous benefits to policyholders. These include relieving them of the burden of complex claims processes and negotiations with insurance companies. They ensure claims are filed promptly and accurately; they help in understanding the intricacies of the insurance policy and work tirelessly to expedite the claims process while securing the maximum possible settlement.

WHAT MAKES PUBLIC INSURANCE ADJUSTING DIFFERENT FROM INSURANCE ADJUSTERS, AGENTS, AND BROKERS

Public insurance adjusters differ significantly from other professionals in the insurance field. Insurance agents and brokers are involved in the sale and management of insurance policies, whereas insurance adjusters, employed by insurance companies, work to evaluate and settle claims from the insurer's perspective. In contrast, public adjusters work exclusively for the policyholder, focusing on maximizing the claim settlement in favor of the insured.

Distinct Responsibilities and Focus of Each Role

It is crucial that you as a public adjuster understand the distinct responsibilities and focus of various roles within the insurance industry. This understanding enables you to effectively navigate the claims process and collaborate or negotiate with other insurance professionals to best serve your clients' interests.

Advocate for Policyholders' Interests

Public insurance adjusters are staunch advocates for policyholders, ensuring that their rights are protected throughout the claims process. They scrutinize the insurance policy to identify all possible avenues for claim recovery and challenge any unfair claim denials or underpayments by insurance companies.

Key Players in the Insurance Ecosystem

The insurance ecosystem is composed of several key players, each with distinct roles and responsibilities. Understanding these roles is crucial, as it enables you to navigate the complexities of the insurance world more effectively.

INSURED INDIVIDUALS AND POLICYHOLDERS

Role of Insured Individuals as Policyholders

Insured individuals, or policyholders, are at the heart of the insurance ecosystem. They enter into a contract with an insurance company to protect themselves against potential financial losses due to unforeseen events, such as accidents, natural disasters, or other calamities. As policyholders, they pay premiums in exchange for the assurance that the insurer will cover their losses under the terms of the policy.

Rights and Responsibilities Within Insurance Contracts

Policyholders have specific rights and responsibilities under their insurance contracts. They are entitled to the protection and benefits stipulated in their policy, provided they adhere to the terms and conditions. This includes paying premiums on time, reporting losses promptly, and providing accurate and complete information during the claims process. Policyholders also have the right to challenge decisions made by their insurance company and seek assistance from public insurance adjusters if they feel their claim has not been adequately addressed.

INSURANCE CARRIERS

Role of Insurance Companies in Underwriting Policies

Insurance carriers, or insurance companies, are organizations that provide risk management to individuals, businesses, and other entities. Their primary role is to underwrite, or assess and take on, the risk presented by policyholders. They determine the terms of coverage, set premium rates, and decide which risks they are willing to insure based on their risk assessment models.

Different Types of Insurance Carriers

There are various types of insurance carriers, ranging from large national companies to smaller regional firms. National insurance carriers typically offer a wide range of insurance products and operate across multiple states, benefiting from a broader pool of risk and resources. On the other hand, regional insurance companies may specialize in specific types of insurance or cater to the unique needs of a particular geographical area. Understanding the differences between these carriers is essential for public adjusters, as it affects how they approach negotiations and claim resolutions for their clients.

In the realm of insurance, understanding the distinction between domestic admitted insurance companies and surplus lines insurance companies is crucial, especially in contexts where complex or high-risk coverage is required. This distinction becomes particularly relevant when considering entities like the Lloyd's Market, which operates in the surplus lines industry.

Domestic admitted insurance companies are insurers that are licensed and regulated by the insurance regulatory authority of the state in which they operate. Being "admitted" means these companies must comply with all state regulations regarding insurance, including solvency standards, policy forms, and rate approvals. These regulations are designed to protect policyholders by ensuring these insurers maintain sufficient financial reserves to pay claims. Policyholders of admitted insurance companies also benefit from state guarantee funds, which provide a safety net in the event of the insurer's insolvency.

In contrast, surplus lines insurance companies, such as those operating in the Lloyd's Market, specialize in underwriting unusual or higher-risk insurance that admitted insurers typically do not cover. These companies are not licensed in the states where they write policies, hence they are not bound by the same regulations as admitted insurers. This regulatory flexibility allows surplus lines insurers to cover unique risks, set customized premiums, and draft specialized insurance policies. However, the lack of stringent regulatory oversight means policyholders do not have the protection of state guarantee funds.

The Lloyd's Market, known for its global presence and capacity to insure complex and specialty risks, operates in this surplus lines space. It offers a marketplace where underwriters can provide coverage for risks that traditional admitted insurers might deem too unusual or hazardous. The expertise and flexibility of surplus lines insurers, like those in the Lloyd's Market, are invaluable in situations where standard insurance solutions are inadequate. However, policyholders must be aware of the differences in regulatory protections when choosing between domestic admitted insurers and surplus lines providers, like the Lloyd's Market.

INSURANCE AGENTS AND BROKERS

Insurance Agents

Insurance agents act as intermediaries between policyholders and insurance companies. Unlike brokers, agents usually have a contractual relationship with specific insurance companies, representing one or more of these firms. They sell policies provided by these insurers and are often seen as the face of the insurance company to the policyholder.

Agents' roles involve not only selling insurance policies but also helping clients understand their insurance needs. They explain the details of various policies, including coverage limits, deductibles, and exclusions. Agents assist in the application process, ensuring all necessary information is gathered and submitted correctly.

One of the key aspects of an agent's role is to maintain ongoing relationships with their clients. This involves regular communication, providing updates on new products or changes in existing policies, and assisting clients with policy renewals. In the event of a claim, agents often play a pivotal role in facilitating the claims process, acting as a liaison between the policyholder and the insurer.

Insurance Brokers

Insurance brokers specialize in selling policies and providing customer service, but their approach is markedly client-centric. Unlike agents who represent insurance companies, brokers represent the interests of the policyholders. They work as independent entities and are not bound to any specific insurance company. This independence allows brokers to scan the insurance market broadly, comparing policies from various insurers to find the best fit for their clients' needs.

Brokers' expertise lies in understanding the complexities of different insurance products and translating them into understandable terms for clients. They guide policyholders through the selection process, helping them understand the nuances of various coverage options. Once a policy is chosen, brokers assist with the application process and provide ongoing support, including answering policy-related questions and helping with claims.

Furthermore, brokers are known for their personalized customer service. They build relationships with clients to understand their unique insurance needs, offering tailored advice and solutions. This client-focused approach ensures policyholders receive coverage that aligns closely with their individual or business risks.

THE CLAIMS PROCESS AND CLAIM INDEMNIFICATION

Navigating the labyrinth of the insurance claims process can be a daunting task for policyholders. This complexity underscores the importance of public insurance adjusters in guiding clients through this intricate procedure. Understanding each phase of the claims process and the crucial role of public insurance adjusters in claim indemnification is essential for those in this profession.

UNDERSTANDING THE CLAIMS PROCESS

The claims process typically unfolds in several stages, beginning with the immediate aftermath of a loss. The first step for a policyholder is to notify their insurance company of the loss, a phase known as the claim initiation or filing. This initial contact should be prompt, as delays can complicate the process. Late notice or reporting of a loss can result in a claim denial, so every effort to report a loss as soon as it occurs is important.

Following the notification, an insurance adjuster is assigned to the claim. When an insurance company faces a claim, it has the option to appoint either a company adjuster or an independent claims adjuster. A company adjuster, also known as a staff adjuster, is a salaried employee of the insurance company. They work exclusively for one insurer and handle claims on their behalf. On the other hand, an independent claims adjuster is not tied to any particular insurance company. They operate independently and are contracted by various insurers to handle claims. The primary difference lies in their employment status and allegiance; company adjusters represent the interests of their employer (the insurance company), while independent adjusters offer a more neutral service, managing claims for multiple insurers without direct employment ties to any. This distinction can influence their approach to claims handling, potentially impacting the assessment and settlement process.

Regardless of the type of adjuster assigned, all first-party property insurance adjusters investigate facts of the loss related to coverage and evaluate the amount of the loss. They review the policy coverages and determine the insurance company's liability. The assessment stage involves promptly examining the damage, interviewing witnesses or involved parties, and gathering relevant information.

After the evaluation, the adjuster presents a claim settlement proposal. This proposal is based on the adjuster's assessment of the damage and the policy terms. If the policyholder accepts this offer, the claim proceeds to the payment stage, culminating in the indemnification of the policyholder.

IMPORTANCE OF DOCUMENTATION AND TIMELY FILING

Thorough documentation and timely filing are pivotal in the claims process. While the insurance company has its own good faith duty to investigate facts of coverage and evaluate the amount of the damages payable, policyholders have post-loss duties required under the policy. Most require the policyholder to document the damage. Public adjusters play a crucial role in the post-loss obligations by comprehensively providing the documentation to support the claim, including obtaining photographs or visual evidence of the loss, repair estimates, and assisting obtaining reports from experts if necessary. This documentation serves as the foundation for the claim and is crucial in establishing the extent of the loss.

Timeliness in filing the claim is equally important. Insurance policies often have strict deadlines for notifying the insurer of a loss. Failing to meet these deadlines, such as filing a proof of loss, can result in denied claims or reduced settlements. Thus, prompt action and detailed record-keeping are essential.

POTENTIAL CHALLENGES AND OBSTACLES

Navigating the insurance claims process is often fraught with challenges and obstacles that can complicate the path to a fair and timely settlement. One of the most common issues encountered is misunderstandings regarding policy coverage. Insurance policies are complex documents, and the nuances in coverage terms can lead to confusion among policyholders about what is and isn't covered. This misunderstanding can result in disputes when a claim is filed, especially if the policyholder's expectations of coverage differ from the insurer's interpretation of the policy.

Disputes over the extent of damage and the value of the loss are also prevalent. Assessing the damage after an event like a fire, theft, or natural disaster can be subjective. The policyholder and the insurance company might have different views on the severity of the damage or the cost of repairs. These disagreements can be about the methods of repair, the necessity of certain repairs, or the valuation of damaged items. Such disputes can significantly delay the claims process as both parties strive to justify their assessments.

Another common challenge is delays in the claims process, which can be caused by several factors. On the insurer's side, extensive investigations into the claim, particularly for large or complex claims, can prolong the process. Insurance companies must ensure the claim is valid and falls within the policy's scope, necessitating a thorough review which can be time-consuming.

From the policyholder's perspective, delays can occur if they are unable to provide the necessary documentation promptly. This documentation is crucial for substantiating the claim and includes evidence of the damage, proof of ownership, and records of the value of the items lost or damaged. Gathering this information can be challenging, especially in the aftermath of a traumatic event. Moreover, if the policyholder fails to provide comprehensive and accurate documentation, the claim may be underpaid or denied.

The complexities of the claims process underscore the value of having skilled professionals, such as public insurance adjusters, to assist policyholders. These experts can help navigate these challenges, ensuring the policyholder's rights are protected and the claim is handled efficiently and fairly. They can clarify policy terms, assist in damage assessment and documentation, and represent the policyholder in negotiations with the insurance company, helping to overcome the obstacles that can arise during the claims process.

THE ROLE OF PUBLIC INSURANCE ADJUSTERS IN CLAIM INDEMNIFICATION

Support Throughout the Claims Process

Public insurance adjusters provide invaluable support to policyholders throughout the claims process. Their role is to represent the policyholder's interests, offering an independent and professional evaluation of the loss.

Expertise in Assessing Damages and Valuing Claims

Public adjusters possess expertise in accurately assessing damages and valuing claims. They conduct thorough inspections of the damage, compile detailed inventories, and use their knowledge to estimate repair costs accurately. Their assessments often uncover damages that the policyholder or the insurance company's adjuster might overlook, ensuring all aspects of the loss are considered.

Negotiating With Insurance Carriers

One of the key roles of public adjusters is negotiating with insurance carriers. They use their understanding of insurance policies and the claims process to advocate for fair compensation. This negotiation is critical, especially in complex claims where the valuation of damages can be subjective or in situations where the initial settlement offer is insufficient.

Public adjusters also assist in navigating the often-confusing language of insurance policies, helping policyholders understand their coverage and rights. They ensure claims are filed correctly and within the required timeframes, reducing the likelihood of disputes or delays.

Securing Fair Compensation for Policyholders

The ultimate goal of public insurance adjusters is to secure fair and just compensation for policyholders. They strive to ensure the settlement reflects the true extent of the loss and that policyholders receive the benefits they are entitled to under their insurance policy. This commitment to fairness and thoroughness is what sets public adjusters apart and makes them an invaluable asset in the claims process.

RICH'S STORY

THE SIGNIFICANCE OF PUBLIC INSURANCE ADJUSTING

As Rich delved deeper into the world of public adjusting, his revelations about the industry's structure and its impact on policyholders grew increasingly profound. "This entire system," he thought to himself, "is so complex, yet so pivotal in times of need. And here at the center of it are public adjusters, the true advocates for policyholders."

He considered how, in contrast to insurance agents and brokers who often represent the insurance companies, public adjusters dedicate themselves solely to the policyholder. "It's a role that flips the typical dynamics of the insurance industry on its head," Rich reflected. He realized that while many see insurance as a routine financial transaction, for those affected by disaster or loss, it's a lifeline, making the role of a public adjuster crucial.

"Public adjusters are more than just claim handlers; they're champions for the underdog," Rich mused, feeling a surge of admiration. The more he learned, the more he saw the gaps in the system that could leave policyholders vulnerable and underserved. "They need someone who not only understands the fine print but who will also stand up and fight for them," he considered, his resolve strengthening.

His exploration of the broader insurance market also opened his eyes to the sheer scale and intricacies of the industry. "So many moving parts, yet so few focus on the real needs of the policyholder," Rich noted with a mix of awe and frustration. Understanding the nuances of claims, from the necessity of meticulous documentation to the intricacies of claim filing deadlines, underscored the value public adjusters bring. "They navigate this maze with expertise, ensuring no detail is missed, no right is overlooked."

Through his journey, Rich developed not just an academic understanding but a heartfelt respect for the mission of public adjusters. "They're not just navigating claims; they're safeguarding futures," he concluded, feeling a profound sense of purpose and a renewed commitment to his new path. His adventure in public adjusting had indeed become a discovery of a hidden treasure trove—the invaluable service these professionals provide to those in their most vulnerable moments.

CHAPTER 2
UNDERSTANDING THE LEGAL AND REGULATORY LANDSCAPE

> In matters of style, swim with the current; in matters of principle, stand like a rock.
>
> THOMAS JEFFERSON

IN THE INTRICATE world of public insurance adjusting, a thorough understanding and strict compliance with legal and regulatory requirements is absolutely essential. This chapter details the multifaceted legal landscape that you must navigate as a public adjuster, highlighting the significance of adhering to these standards not only for legal compliance but also for maintaining the highest ethical standards in the profession.

As a public adjuster, you play a crucial role in the insurance industry, acting as an advocate for policyholders during the often complex and stressful process of filing and negotiating insurance claims. Your work demands a deep knowledge of insurance policies, damage assessment, and negotiation skills. However, it is equally important for you to understand the legal and regulatory framework you operate within. This chapter elucidates these legal and regulatory considerations to provide you with the knowledge you need to operate lawfully and ethically as a public adjuster.

THE LEGAL AND REGULATORY LANDSCAPE

The realm of public insurance adjusting is governed by a complex and varied legal framework, which is crucial for adjusters to understand and navigate effectively. This section explores the intricacies of the laws, regulations, and industry-specific guidelines that shape the practice of public insurance adjusting.

Overview of the Legal Framework Governing Public Insurance Adjusters

Public insurance adjusters are regulated primarily at the state level, with each state having its own set of laws and regulations. These laws are designed to protect policyholders and ensure adjusters operate in a fair, ethical, and professional manner. The legal framework typically covers aspects such as licensing requirements, conduct of business, fee structures, and the adjuster's fiduciary responsibilities to their clients.

◆ **Licensing Requirements**

Most states require public adjusters to be licensed. This process often involves passing a written examination, meeting educational prerequisites, and adhering to ethical standards. Some states also require background checks and proof of financial responsibility, such as surety bonds. We have added an Appendix at the end of this book to help guide you with specifics if you are not currently a licensed public insurance adjuster.

◆ **Conduct of Business**

State laws regulate how adjusters can solicit business, interact with policyholders, and negotiate with insurance companies. These regulations are designed to prevent fraudulent practices and ensure adjusters act in the best interest of their clients.

◆ **Fee Structures**

Many states have regulations governing the fees public adjusters can charge. These may include caps on fees as a percentage of the claim settlement and stipulations on how and when fees can be collected.

FAMILIARIZE YOURSELF WITH INSURANCE LAWS AND REGULATIONS THAT IMPACT CLAIM HANDLING

Insurance laws and regulations are the bedrock upon which the practice of claim handling is built. Public adjusters must be well-versed in these laws to effectively advocate for their clients.

State Insurance Codes

Each state has its own insurance code which outlines the legal framework for all aspects of insurance within that state. These codes cover a wide range of topics, including policy terms, claim handling procedures, and adjuster conduct.

Regulatory Guidelines

In addition to statutory laws, states often issue regulatory guidelines that provide more detailed instructions on how laws should be interpreted and applied in specific situations. These guidelines can be crucial in understanding the nuances of claim handling.

Case Law

Judicial decisions in insurance cases also play a significant role in shaping the practice of claim handling. Public adjusters should be aware of relevant case law, as it can provide valuable precedents and interpretations of insurance statutes and regulations.

Public adjusters must be well-versed in the laws and regulations that pertain to the handling of insurance claims and the advocacy of policyholder rights. This includes understanding the nuances of insurance policies, the claims process, and the rights of policyholders under the law.

Insurance Policies

Adjusters must have a deep understanding of various types of insurance policies, including homeowners, commercial property, and business interruption policies. This knowledge is crucial for interpreting coverage, exclusions, and policy limits. Modern insurance forms are constantly changing, and public adjusters must be constantly committed to learning how new policy language impacts coverages available to policyholder clients.

"RTFP"— Read The Full Policy — is a phrase which is paramount to public adjusters because each policy provides different terms and conditions impacting coverage and placing duties on policyholders. Public adjusters have to be experts in understanding and deciphering how policy language can provide the maximum amount of coverage benefit to policyholders.

Claims Process

Adjusters must be familiar with the procedural aspects of filing and negotiating claims. This includes knowledge of timelines for filing claims, documentation requirements, and the process and deadlines for disputing claim decisions.

Policyholder Rights

Public adjusters advocate for policyholders, and as such, they must be aware of the legal rights of policyholders. This includes understanding laws related to bad faith insurance practices and the policyholder's right to fair treatment and prompt payment of claims. It is illegal for public adjusters to practice law. However, public adjusters must know intimately how laws and regulations impact every claim on a state-by-state basis. An intimate knowledge of state insurance law is a pre-requisite to a public adjuster properly adjusting an insurance claim.

RESEARCHING INDUSTRY-SPECIFIC GUIDELINES AND STANDARDS TO ENSURE COMPLIANCE

In addition to state laws and regulations, public adjusters must also be aware of industry-specific guidelines and standards. These may include best practices established by professional associations, ethical codes, and guidelines for specific types of claims.

Professional Associations

Professional Trade Organizations, such as the National Association of Public Insurance Adjusters (NAPIA), provide resources, education, and ethical guidelines for adjusters. Membership in such regional and national public adjuster associations can be a valuable resource for staying informed about industry standards and changes in regulations which impact claim handling and regulatory compliance.

Please visit the *Claim Your Success* site for links to NAPIA and other relevant trade associations.

Each state has its own ethics codes. Public adjusters must know and adhere to the applicable state code or risk administrative penalties that could include losing a public adjusting license.

For example, Florida has a Code of Ethics. Public adjusters in Florida are licensed by the Department of Financial Services and have several ethical requirements they must meet due to the nature of the service they provide. These regulatory rules are found in Florida's Administrative Code and provide ethical duties which are like many other states which license public adjusting.

Specialized Guidelines

For certain types of claims, such as natural disaster claims or large-scale property losses, there may be specialized laws, guidelines, and procedures that adjusters need to follow. Staying informed about these guidelines, which are often emphasized in bulletins from state insurance offices, ensures adjusters can effectively manage complex claims.

Department of Insurance Bulletins

Bulletins are official communications issued by state insurance departments to provide guidance, clarification, or instructions regarding insurance laws, regulations, and practices. These bulletins can significantly impact public adjusters by updating or interpreting regulatory requirements, announcing changes in policy or enforcement priorities, and providing insights into best practices. Public adjusters must stay informed about these bulletins, as they can directly affect how adjusters handle claims, interact with policyholders, and comply with state-specific legal and ethical standards. Ignoring these bulletins could lead to non-compliance, legal challenges, or professional misconduct.

UNDERSTAND THE RIGHTS AND RESPONSIBILITIES OF POLICYHOLDERS AND INSURANCE CARRIERS

A comprehensive understanding of the rights and responsibilities of both policyholders and insurance carriers is essential for public adjusters.

Policyholder Rights

Policyholders have certain rights under their insurance policies and state laws, such as the right to a fair and timely assessment of their claims, the right to be informed about the status of their claim, and the right to challenge decisions made by insurance carriers. Policyholders may have legal rights which public adjusters are required to know. They should suggest to the policyholder that legal counsel should be consulted.

Public Adjusters should be familiar with Model Unfair Claims laws promulgated by the NAIC. Many of these consumer protection laws are found in state regulations. Most states have enacted a version of this model law. Called the Unfair Claims Settlement Practices Act, it protects insurance buyers from unjust behavior by insurers in the claims settlement process. Specifics of the law vary from state to state. Unfair Claims Settlement Practices Acts (UCSPA) are not federal law. Instead, they are enforced by individual state insurance departments. Some states provide a private right of action by policyholders under these laws.

Insurance Carrier Responsibilities

Insurance carriers are obligated to act in good faith, to investigate claims promptly and thoroughly, and to provide clear and reasonable explanations for claim decisions. They must also adhere to the terms of the insurance policies they issue and comply with state insurance laws.

COMPLY WITH REQUIREMENTS RELATED TO CLAIMS ASSESSMENT, NEGOTIATION, AND SETTLEMENT

The final stage of the claims process involves assessment, negotiation, and settlement, all of which are governed by specific legal and regulatory requirements.

Claims Assessment

The assessment of a claim involves investigating the facts relating to coverage, evaluating the damage or loss, and determining the appropriate payout under the policy terms. This process must be conducted in a manner that is fair, thorough, prompt, and in accordance with the policy provisions and applicable laws.

Negotiation

Negotiation is a critical skill for public adjusters. They must negotiate with insurance carriers to reach a settlement that is in the best interest of the policyholder. This process requires a deep understanding of insurance law, strong communication skills, and an ability to advocate effectively for the client.

Settlement

The settlement of a claim is the culmination of the claims process. It involves agreeing on the amount to be paid to the policyholder. Settlements must comply with the terms of the insurance policy and be consistent with state laws and regulations. Public adjusters play a key role in ensuring settlements are fair and equitable.

COMPLYING WITH INDUSTRY REGULATIONS, ETHICAL STANDARDS, AND PROFESSIONALISM

For public insurance adjusters, adherence to industry regulations and ethical standards is not just a legal requirement but a cornerstone of professional integrity and reputation. Chapter 14: Ethical Practices delves into the ethical guidelines that govern the conduct of public insurance adjusters and the best practices for claims handling.

Professionalism in public adjusting is a multifaceted concept that encompasses a range of behaviors, ethics, and practices essential for effectively serving policyholders and maintaining the integrity of the profession. At its core, professionalism in this field involves a commitment to ethical conduct, expertise in insurance matters, and a dedication to client advocacy. For more information, see Chapter 13: Professional Development.

LICENSING AND CERTIFICATION REQUIREMENTS

In the field of public insurance adjusting, licensing and certification are not merely formalities; they are essential components that ensure the credibility, knowledge, and ethical conduct of professionals. This section delves into the various aspects of licensing and certification requirements for public insurance adjusters, their qualifications, the examination process, continuing education obligations, and the regulatory bodies involved in overseeing these processes.

We have added an Appendix at the end of this book to help guide you with specifics if you are not currently a licensed public insurance adjuster.

RICH'S STORY

UNDERSTANDING THE LEGAL AND REGULATORY LANDSCAPE

As Rich embarked on his journey to become a licensed public adjuster, he approached the legal and regulatory landscape with a mix of curiosity and determination. The process of obtaining his license, while demanding, proved to be an enlightening experience that deepened his understanding of the industry.

Rich discovered that each state had its own set of requirements for public adjusters. He methodically researched the regulations, educational prerequisites, and examination processes for his state. While the volume of information was substantial, Rich found that his experience in the insurance industry provided a solid foundation for understanding many of the concepts.

He dedicated time to studying insurance laws, ethics, and claim handling procedures, supplementing his existing knowledge with new insights. Rich attended seminars and engaged in online courses, finding that much of the material reinforced what he had learned through practical experience.

When exam day arrived, Rich felt well-prepared. The test covered a wide range of topics from policy interpretation to state-specific laws. While some questions required careful consideration, Rich found that his combination of study and real-world experience allowed him to navigate the exam with confidence.

After obtaining his license, Rich embraced the ongoing nature of professional development in the field. He viewed the continuing education requirements not as a burden, but as an opportunity to stay current in an ever-evolving industry. He regularly attended workshops and conferences, often finding that these events provided valuable insights that he could apply directly to his work.

As his business expanded, Rich faced the challenge of understanding and complying with regulations in different states. He approached this task systematically, researching the licensing requirements for each new state he entered and developing a system to track various renewal deadlines and Continuing Education requirements.

Rich's commitment to understanding and adhering to the legal and regulatory landscape became a cornerstone of his practice. It allowed him to navigate complex claims with assurance and provide reliable guidance to his clients, reinforcing his decision to pursue public adjusting as a career.

PART TWO
SETTING UP YOUR PUBLIC ADJUSTING FIRM

CHAPTER 3
DEVELOPING & IMPLEMENTING A BUSINESS PLAN

A goal without a plan is just a wish.

ANTOINE DE SAINT-EXUPÉRY

IN THE WORLD OF ENTREPRENEURSHIP, the term "business plan" often conjures up images of startups seeking funding or aspiring entrepreneurs outlining their grand (and unreasonable) visions for the future. While it's true that business plans are a fundamental component of launching a new venture, their importance extends far beyond the realm of startups. Business plans play a vital role in the success and growth of both new and existing businesses. This chapter explores the significance of a business plan for your public adjusting business and explore how it can serve as a road map to your success.

One of the most common misconceptions in the business world is that business plans are solely the domain of startups seeking investors or lenders. While it's true that startups often use business plans to secure funding, the value of a well-crafted business plan goes far beyond this initial purpose. A business plan is a dynamic document that outlines a company's goals, strategies, and operational plans, providing a clear road map for the future. It is a tool for strategic thinking and decision-making, and it is just as relevant for established businesses as it is for startups.

In the context of public adjusting businesses, entrepreneurs often underestimate the importance of a business plan once they have launched their company. They may believe that their industry expertise and experience are sufficient to guide them. However, even the most seasoned professionals can benefit from the clarity and direction that a well-thought-out business plan provides.

For existing businesses, there is another misconception – the idea that once a business plan is created, it is set in stone. In reality, a business plan should be a living document that evolves alongside the business itself. The industry, market conditions, insurance regulations, services you offer, and business goals can change over time, necessitating updates and refinements to the plan. It may be best to revisit your business plan every two to three years and update as needed.

Think of your business plan as a compass. While it provides a clear direction, it also allows for adjustments as you navigate through changing landscapes. Regularly reviewing and updating your business plan ensures that your strategies remain relevant, your goals stay achievable, and your business remains agile in response to new opportunities and challenges.

Whether you're launching a new public adjusting business or managing an existing one, a clear and concise business plan offers numerous benefits that can significantly impact your success:

Clarity of Purpose

A well-defined business plan helps you and your team understand the purpose and objectives of your business. It aligns everyone with a common vision, fostering a sense of purpose and direction.

Strategic Decision-Making

Your business plan serves as a strategic guide, helping you make informed decisions. When faced with choices, you can refer back to your plan to assess whether they align with your overall goals.

Financial Planning

A business plan includes financial projections and budgets, enabling you to manage your finances effectively. It helps you monitor cash flow, set financial targets, and identify potential financial bottlenecks.

Resource Allocation

Knowing where you're headed allows you to allocate resources – both human and financial – more efficiently. You can focus on areas that will have the most significant impact on your business.

Risk Mitigation

By outlining potential risks and contingency plans in your business plan, you are better prepared to handle unexpected challenges. This proactive approach minimizes the impact of setbacks.

Communication Tool

A well-crafted business plan can be shared with stakeholders, including employees, investors, lenders, and potential partners. It communicates your business's value proposition and strategic direction effectively.

Now that we've established the importance of a business plan for public insurance adjusting businesses, let's dive into the essential components that should be included in your plan, starting with defining your mission, vision, and goals.

DEVELOPING THE BUSINESS PLAN

At the heart of every successful public adjusting business is a clear sense of purpose and a set of core values. The mission and values of your business define its identity and provide a foundation upon which all decisions and actions are based. They guide your interactions with clients, employees, and partners and shape the culture of your organization.

Mission Statement

Your mission statement is a concise expression of your business's purpose. It should reflect why your public adjusting business exists and the positive impact it aims to make on policyholders' lives. Crafting a compelling mission statement is an essential step in defining your business's identity and purpose.

For example, your business' mission statement might read:

> Our mission is to advocate for and protect commercial enterprises during their most challenging property losses, leveraging deep industry expertise to ensure maximum claim recovery and business continuity. Through unwavering integrity, technical excellence, and sophisticated claim strategies, we champion our clients' rights to full indemnification, enabling them to rebuild and thrive.

This mission statement works because it:

- Clearly identifies the target market (commercial enterprises)
- Emphasizes the value proposition (expertise in large loss claims)
- Highlights key differentiators (sophisticated strategies, technical excellence)

- Communicates the ultimate benefit (business continuity and recovery)
- Reinforces professional values (integrity, expertise)

Your core values are the guiding principles that underpin your business's culture and behavior. They shape how you conduct business, make decisions, and interact with clients and partners. Identifying and communicating your core values is crucial for maintaining consistency and integrity in your operations.

In the book *Clockwork* by Mike Michalowicz, two fundamental concepts are brought to the forefront, particularly in the context of public adjusters as analyzed by Lynette Young, Clockwork Certified Partner.™ These are the "Big Promise" and the "Queen Bee Role" (QBR). These are both essential for formulating a strategic framework for public adjusters to enhance their business operations and client service.

◆ **The Big Promise**

This concept loosely reflects your Mission Statement and focuses on the core commitment a business makes to its customers. For public adjusters, the Big Promise could be "ensuring fair and maximum compensation for clients' insurance claims." This promise forms the foundation of their business plan, guiding their service offerings, customer engagement strategies, and overall mission. It's a commitment to reliability, expertise, and advocacy in navigating the often-complex world of insurance claims.

◆ **The Queen Bee Role (QBR)**

The QBR is the most crucial function or task within a company that supports and fulfills the Big Promise. In the context of public adjusters, the QBR could be the "thorough policy assessment and documentation of damages for insurance claims." This function is vital because it directly impacts the effectiveness and credibility of the claim process. The business plan must prioritize and protect the QBR, ensuring that all resources, training, and processes are aligned to support it effectively. Note that the QBR is a function, not a person or job title. In nature, the queen bee services the most critical function for the health and longevity of the hive — laying eggs. If she is compromised and cannot fulfill this function, she is replaced (sometimes rather violently.) It is the function that is critical, not her specifically.

Incorporating these concepts into their business plan, public adjusters can create a focused, client-centered approach. The Big Promise serves as the north star for all business activities, ensuring that every action taken is aligned with delivering on this commitment. The emphasis on the QBR ensures that the most critical aspect of their service — accurate and comprehensive claim assessment — is given the utmost attention and resources.

By aligning their business plan with the Big Promise and effectively executing and protecting the QBR, public adjusters can establish a reputation for excellence and reliability. This approach not only benefits their clients but also sets the foundation for a sustainable and successful business in the competitive field of insurance adjustment.

SETTING AMBITIOUS YET REALISTIC SHORT-TERM AND LONG-TERM GOALS

Goals are the driving force behind your business's growth and success. They provide a road map for achieving your vision and fulfilling your mission. Effective goals are both ambitious and realistic, challenging your business to strive for excellence while remaining attainable.

Short-Term Goals

Short-term goals typically cover a one- to three-year timeframe. They should be specific, measurable, achievable, relevant, and time-bound (SMART). Short-term goals might include increasing your client base by a certain percentage, expanding your service offerings, or improving customer satisfaction scores.

Long-Term Goals

Long-term goals extend beyond the three-year mark and often encompass a five- to ten-year horizon. These goals should align with your business's overarching vision and mission. Long-term goals could involve achieving a certain level of market dominance, expanding into new geographic areas, or diversifying revenue streams with additional service offerings.

Remember that goals should be adaptable and subject to periodic review and adjustment as your business evolves. They should challenge you and your team to strive for continuous improvement and growth.

IMPLEMENTING YOUR PLAN

Implementing your business plan is where the rubber meets the road. It's the phase where you transform your strategic road map into action, monitor progress, and adapt to changes and challenges along the way. Here we will explore the essential steps of implementing your business plan, including setting action steps and timelines, monitoring and evaluation, and adapting to changes and challenges.

For a public adjusting business, you will want to consider two road maps: business and claim. Working an insurance claim has an entire set of rules and constraints entirely separate from running a business. In this section we are covering strategic road maps for your business; in Chapter 10: Claims Handling and Negotiation Processes we cover designing and implementing a claim workflow process.

To develop your strategic road map, you'll need to break down the strategic road map into actionable steps:

- Implement a system to monitor and measure the progress of your business plan;
- Make necessary adjustments as your business evolves; and
- Embrace a flexible mindset and adapt strategies as needed.

Let's dive into the finer points of each step.

Break Down the Strategic Road Map into Actionable Steps

To successfully implement your business plan, you must break down your strategic road map into actionable steps. These are the specific tasks and activities that need to be completed to move your business closer to its goals.

◆ **Task Identification**

Review your road map and identify the individual tasks required for each strategy and action plan. Ensure that each task is well-defined and achievable. Tasks may include larger tasks such as client acquisition or smaller tasks such as weekly expense reporting.

◆ **Responsibilities**

Assign responsibilities for each task to team members or individuals within your organization. Clearly define who is accountable for each task to ensure accountability. When a task has no owner or expected outcomes, that task does not get completed.

◆ **Dependencies**

Recognize any dependencies between tasks. Some tasks may need to be completed before others can start. Understanding these dependencies helps you create a logical sequence of actions.

◆ **Set Clear Deadlines and Milestones for Each Task**

Once you've identified the tasks, it's crucial to set clear deadlines and milestones. These timeframes help ensure that progress is being made according to the plan and allow for timely adjustments if necessary.

◆ **Task Deadlines**

Assign specific deadlines to each task. These deadlines should be realistic and take into account the time, resources, potential obstacles, and legal deadlines associated with each task. Although a task itself may only take 30 minutes, finding time to focus on that task for 30 minutes may take two weeks. Be sure to consider task duration as well as capacity when assigning deadlines.

◆ **Milestones**

Define milestones within your timeline. Milestones are significant achievements or points of progress that serve as markers for tracking your overall progress. They can be tied to specific goals or objectives. Wanting to "increase your client base" is fine but attaching metrics is better. "Increase net income by 15% in 12 months" is better!

◆ **Completion Criteria**

Clearly outline the criteria that determine when a task or milestone is considered completed. This ensures that there is no ambiguity about the progress being made.

◆ **Assign Responsibilities to Team Members and Track Progress**

Effective implementation of your business plan requires a team effort. Assigning responsibilities and tracking progress ensures that everyone is aligned and accountable.

◆ **Team Alignment**

Communicate responsibilities to your team members or relevant stakeholders. Ensure that everyone understands their role and how their contributions fit into the larger plan.

◆ **Progress Tracking**

Implement a system for tracking claim progress, such as ClaimWizard. This will give you immediate and transparent status on how every claim in your company is progressing.

◆ **Accountability**

Hold team members accountable for their assigned tasks. Encourage open communication and provide support when needed to overcome obstacles.

IMPLEMENT A SYSTEM TO MONITOR AND MEASURE THE PROGRESS OF THE BUSINESS PLAN

Monitoring and evaluation are essential for gauging the effectiveness of your business plan implementation. This involves creating a system to track and measure progress against your goals and objectives.

Key Performance Indicators (KPIs)

Key Performance Indicators (KPIs) are quantifiable measures that are used to gauge the performance of a business, team, or individual in achieving key objectives. These metrics help organizations assess the effectiveness of their operations and strategies in real time. For a public insurance adjusting firm, relevant KPIs might include:

- Revenue Growth: This KPI tracks the increase or decrease in the firm's earnings over time, helping to gauge financial health and market expansion.
- Client Acquisition Rates: This measures the rate at which new clients are brought on board, indicating the effectiveness of marketing and outreach strategies.
- Customer Satisfaction Scores: Often gathered through surveys post-service, these scores provide insight into client happiness and service quality, which are critical for reputation and client retention.
- Project Completion Timelines: This tracks how efficiently claims or projects are completed, showing the operational efficiency and effectiveness of the team.

Objectives and Key Results (OKRs)

Objectives and Key Results (OKRs) are a framework for setting goals and tracking outcomes within an organization. OKRs consist of an objective—a clearly defined goal—and one or more key results—specific measures used to track the achievement of that objective. The objective is ambitious and acts as a motivator for a team, while the key results are measurable and indicate progress toward the objective. Here's how OKRs might be structured for the same firm:

A. Objective: Increase market presence in the state by 25% by the end of the fiscal year.
    - Key Result 1: Achieve a 20% year-over-year increase in revenue.
    - Key Result 2: Grow the client base by 30% through targeted marketing campaigns.
    - Key Result 3: Maintain a customer satisfaction score of at least 90%.

B. Objective: Streamline claims processing to improve efficiency and customer satisfaction.
    - Key Result 1: Reduce average project completion timeline from 60 days to 45 days.
    - Key Result 2: Achieve a customer satisfaction score of 95% for claim resolution processes.
    - Key Result 3: Implement a new training program to enhance adjuster expertise and efficiency.

OKRs help teams focus efforts on impactful activities and drive progress in strategic areas, while KPIs provide the metrics to monitor these efforts. Together, they form a robust framework for strategic management and operational improvement.

Conduct Regular Reviews and Evaluations to Assess Performance

Regular reviews and evaluations are crucial for assessing the performance of your business plan and identifying areas that may require adjustment or improvement.

Frequency

Determine how often you will conduct reviews and evaluations. This could be monthly, quarterly, or annually, depending on your business's needs.

Performance Analysis

Analyze the data collected and compare it to your benchmarks. Assess whether you are on track to meet your goals or if there are any areas of concern.

Identifying Successes and Challenges

Celebrate successes and acknowledge areas where you've excelled. Simultaneously, identify challenges or setbacks that need to be addressed.

Feedback and Insights

Gather feedback from team members and stakeholders involved in the implementation process. Their insights can provide valuable perspectives on what's working and what can be improved.

Make Necessary Adjustments and Modifications as the Business Evolves

Adaptation is a key component of successful business plan implementation. As your business evolves and market conditions change, you must be prepared to make necessary adjustments and modifications to your plan.

Flexibility

Embrace a flexible mindset that is open to change. Understand that not all aspects of your plan may go according to initial expectations, and that's okay.

Contingency Plans

Refer to your contingency plans when faced with unexpected challenges. These plans outline how to address obstacles and ensure that you can pivot when necessary.

Continuous Improvement

Continuously seek opportunities for improvement and growth. This might involve optimizing processes, refining strategies, or exploring new market segments.

ANTICIPATE POTENTIAL OBSTACLES AND DEVELOP CONTINGENCY PLANS

Effective implementation also involves anticipating potential obstacles and having contingency plans in place to address them. Contingency planning helps mitigate risks and ensures that your business can adapt to unexpected challenges. Here's how it can be broken down:

Risk Assessment

Risk assessment is a systematic process used to identify, analyze, and evaluate the risks involved in achieving business objectives. It helps in understanding the likelihood and potential impact of identified risks. Steps include:

- Identifying Risks: This involves recognizing the threats that could negatively affect resources or lead to the failure of objectives. In public adjusting, this could be technological failures, human error, or legal changes affecting claim processes.
- Analyzing Risks: This step assesses the likelihood of each risk occurring and its potential impact on the business. This helps in prioritizing the risks based on their severity.
- Evaluating Risks: This involves deciding which risks need to be addressed and determining the best methods to manage them based on their priority and the company's risk appetite.

Contingency Strategies

Contingency strategies are specific plans developed for a

rapid and effective response should any identified risk materialize. These strategies are essential for ensuring business continuity. For each risk, a contingency strategy might include:

- Preventative Measures: Actions taken to prevent a risk from occurring.
- Mitigation Measures: Steps to minimize the impact of a risk if it cannot be avoided.
- Response Plans: Detailed actions on how to deal with the aftermath of a risk event to quickly restore normal operations.

Resource Allocation

Proper resource allocation ensures that adequate resources (time, budget, personnel) are available to implement contingency plans effectively. This includes:

- Budgetary Allocations: Setting aside funds specifically for crisis management or unexpected situations.
- Team Support: Ensuring there are enough trained personnel available to execute contingency plans. This might involve cross-training employees or hiring temporary workers.
- Tools and Technology: Investing in the right tools and technology that can help manage or mitigate risks, such as upgraded software for data security in the case of cybersecurity threats.

By integrating these elements—risk assessment, contingency strategies, and resource allocation—into your business planning, you can create a robust framework that enhances resilience against uncertainties, ensuring that your firm can continue to operate effectively even under adverse conditions.

EMBRACE A FLEXIBLE MINDSET AND ADAPT STRATEGIES AS NEEDED

Flexibility is a valuable trait when it comes to implementing your business plan. Business landscapes are dynamic, and your ability to adapt strategies as needed is essential for long-term success.

Market Changes

Stay attuned to changes in the market, industry trends, laws, and shifts in customer behavior. Be prepared to adjust your strategies to meet evolving needs.

Feedback Loop

Create a feedback loop within your organization that encourages team members to share insights and suggest improvements. An open dialogue can lead to innovative solutions.

Pivot When Necessary

Don't hesitate to pivot when circumstances warrant it. Whether it's a change in client preferences, competitive pressures, or economic shifts, be ready to adapt your strategies accordingly.

Continuously Seeking Opportunities for Improvement and Growth

Successful implementation is not just about overcoming challenges; it's also about seeking opportunities for improvement and growth.

Continuous Learning

Encourage a culture of continuous learning within your organization. Invest in ongoing training and development for your team to stay ahead in your industry.

Innovation

Explore innovative solutions and technologies that can enhance your services or streamline your processes. Staying innovative can give you a competitive edge.

Feedback Integration

Actively integrate feedback from clients and stakeholders into your business practices. Their insights can lead to refinements and improvements.

Implementing your business plan is a dynamic and ongoing process that requires diligence, adaptability, and a commitment to continuous improvement. By setting clear action steps and timelines, monitoring progress, and being prepared to adapt to changes and challenges, you position your public insurance adjusting business for long-term success.

Remember that the implementation phase is not the end of your journey; it's the beginning of a cycle of continuous growth and refinement. In the chapters that follow, we will explore strategies for client advocacy, operational excellence, and sustainable growth to help you further develop and succeed in your public insurance adjusting business.

FINANCING THE BUSINESS STRATEGY

When you're stepping into the world of public adjusting, having a solid grasp on your financial landscape is absolutely essential. Think of it as crafting a road map that guides you through the financial wilderness of starting and running your business. Let's delve into the nitty-gritty of creating a financial plan that not only keeps your business afloat but also propels it toward sustainable growth.

Start-Up Costs: Laying the Foundation

The first step is to lay down the financial foundation of your business. Identifying your start-up costs is like assembling the pieces of a puzzle. It's about understanding every little expense that goes into making your dream a reality. From the licensing fees that officially kickstart your journey, to creating a brand that resonates with the professional vibe of your business, every detail counts. Don't forget about the nuts and bolts — equipment, insurance to safeguard your venture, and initial marketing expenses to shout your brand from the rooftops. It's about being meticulous, leaving no stone unturned because these initial investments set the stage for your business's future.

Operational Expenses: Keeping the Lights On

Now, imagine your business is a well-oiled machine. Operational expenses are the oil that keeps this machine running smoothly. It's crucial to estimate the costs of keeping your business in motion day after day. Think about the salaries for the talented individuals on your team, the rent for your office space that becomes a second home, and the utilities that keep the lights on and the computers humming. Software subscriptions to streamline your operations and ongoing marketing costs to keep your brand visible are also part of the mix. Breaking down these expenses into fixed (those that stay the same, like rent) and variable (those that can fluctuate, like marketing costs) can help you plan better and ensure that your business operates without a hitch.

Revenue Projections: Charting Your Financial Future

Developing revenue projections is akin to gazing into a crystal ball, but with a lot more data and a bit less mysticism. It's about taking an educated guess on how your business will perform financially. Base these projections on solid ground — your pricing strategy that's competitive yet fair, thorough market research that tells you where your potential clients are, and a well-thought-out sales and marketing plan that outlines how you'll reach your audience. While optimism is a great trait, realism is your best friend here. Consider various scenarios, from the sunny days of a best-case scenario to the stormy ones of a worst-case scenario. This doesn't just prepare you for the future; it arms you with the knowledge to navigate it.

Crafting a financial plan for your public adjusting business is about diving deep into the details, asking the hard questions, and preparing for every possibility. It's a blend of caution and ambition, allowing you to dream big while keeping your feet firmly on the ground. This plan isn't just a document — it's a living, breathing guide that evolves as your business grows. With each step, each decision, and each milestone, you're not just running a business; you're building a legacy. And it all starts with understanding the numbers, embracing the process, and steering your business toward a bright and prosperous future.

Create a Realistic Budget That Aligns with the Business's Goals and Resources

Creating a realistic budget is akin to drawing a map for a treasure hunt. It guides you through the financial landscape of your public adjusting business, ensuring you stay on the right path to reach your goals. Let's walk through the steps to craft a budget that not only reflects your business's ambitions but also its current means.

Revenue and Expense Forecast: Charting Your Financial Course

Begin by merging your revenue projections with your expense estimates. This exercise isn't just about putting numbers on paper; it's about painting a picture of your financial future, whether it's month-by-month or year-by-year. This forecast becomes your compass, showing you how your business is expected to perform financially over time. It's about setting benchmarks, celebrating when you exceed them, and strategizing when you don't.

Cash Flow Management: Keeping the Lifeblood Flowing

Think of cash flow as the lifeblood of your business. Effective cash flow management ensures that this lifeblood keeps circulating, supporting the vital functions of your business. It's about having enough in the tank to keep the engine running during slow periods and to fuel growth opportunities when they arise. Managing your cash flow isn't just about survival; it's about thriving, allowing you to invest in new ventures and navigate through the ebbs and flows of business with confidence.

Contingency Planning: Preparing for the Unexpected

Life, as in business, is full of surprises. Including a contingency fund in your budget is like packing an umbrella for a sunny day; it might feel unnecessary until the weather turns. This buffer is your financial safety net, designed to catch you when unexpected expenses crop up or when revenue doesn't flow as anticipated. It's about being prepared, ensuring that unforeseen challenges don't throw your business off course.

Regular Monitoring: Staying on Track

Setting a budget is only the beginning. The real magic happens in the regular review and adjustment of this budget. It's a dynamic tool, not a static document. By regularly monitoring your financial performance against your projections, you can pivot as needed, seizing new opportunities or mitigating unforeseen risks. It's about staying responsive, agile, and informed, allowing you to steer your business towards success with precision.

WHAT CLAIM FEES TO CHARGE

How much should you charge your client? We get that question several times a week from brand new public adjusters. For every public adjusting company in Florida that I talk to, six more from Texas ask what the Florida folks charge. So, what should YOU charge?

The short answer: *it depends.*

In reality, the contingency fee you charge for your claim work varies due to the state you are adjusting in (fee cap may apply), the type of peril you are working (declared state of emergency), and what the market will tolerate in your area. I've seen ranges from 3% to 10% upwards to 25% and even 35% in Canada and Australia.

Large loss claims may charge less due to the sheer monetary value of the case, and "churn and burn" low-value loss claims may charge a more standard fee due to the time commitment involved.

Full-service public adjusting companies that handle a claim entirely — from filing and origination, estimation and inventory, expert reports, and vendor coordination to processing mortgage checks and collecting recoverable deprecation — can justify charging their full fee.

If you are offering a subset of first-party claims services — such as adjusting-only, estimating, contents inventory, or expert reporting — you will most likely charge a reduced contingency fee, a flat fee, or a charge based on time and expenses.

Appraisal and umpire work are a class of their own when it comes to fees. Better yet, contact the *Insurance Appraisal and Umpire Association (IAUA),* network with professionals, and ASK!

Public Adjuster Fees

The more popular question is "how much do other public adjusters earn from company fees?" Again, this ranges due to multiple factors.

The overwhelming majority of public adjusters working for another person's company are paid on contingency, just as the company is. While overly common, I've seen "staff" public adjusters that are paid on salary and don't receive any monies based on settlement loss amounts and company fees.

Generally, when there is one public adjuster assigned to a claim, their fees range from 35% to 50 percent.

The higher-end is usually reserved for public adjusters that are also owners of the company or those who bring in their own claims to the company. Areas with high competition for good public adjusters will pay a premium to recruit and keep good talent.

Apprentice Fees

Apprentices can expect to earn fees of 10% to 25% per claim, again, based on their experience. Public adjusters that are brand new to the industry under a licensed apprenticeship will earn the lower end of the fee (or a flat fee per claim) while people that have industry experience will earn higher amounts, even equal to the public adjuster rate, depending on their negotiation skills with the company.

When an apprentice ages up and gets their full public adjuster license, they are generally increased to the standard public adjuster fee for that company.

Sales Representative Fees

Some public adjusting companies separate out the job functions of sales and adjusting. For some companies, this arrangement can work quite well. It gives the public adjuster the ability to focus on actually adjusting claims and lets the sales rep shake hands and get ink on contracts.

Situations like this allow the sales rep to close more deals as they are not spending their time adjusting claims, so they actually bring in MORE claims. It becomes a volume play for them. So, even at a typical 5% to 10% of the company fee, they can earn big bucks. In this case, a public adjuster may make slightly less in fees to compensate, but in turn, they aren't knocking on doors looking for a sale and have more claims in their pipeline.

Estimator and Vendor Fees

Per-claim fees for estimators and other vendors such as contents adjusters, expert reports, and exception circumstances such as appraisers and umpires can vary wildly.

Office and Executive Fees

While not common (but highly recommended by us!), some public adjusting companies purposely carve a percentage from each claim fee to cover their office expenses. Since your office staff is not paid a claim commission, their paycheck needs to come from someplace. Rent, phone bill, marketing, software, bookkeeping, taxes, your insurance... all need to be covered. Rather than see what is left over from a claim fee, it may be a better strategy to carve out a percentage directly from each claim fee so that you have an amount to forecast and budget against.

The overwhelming number of public adjusting company owners adjust and will pull their compensation in various ways. What I'm covering here is not any type of owners draw or profit-sharing from the company, but rather a per-claim amount that they receive.

Adjuster/owners may pull a standard (or slightly higher-than-standard) adjuster fee from each company fee. Sometimes they just take 'whatever is left over' and work it all out before the next Tax Day.

A tactic I really like is pulling an Executive Fee from each claim (typically 5% to 10%) that goes into a bucket for the owners to draw a salary from. This means even claims they don't work have guaranteed owner profit built-in.

Your Rates May Vary

You may know of rates much higher or lower than what I've outlined. That's the beauty of the public adjusting industry. None of it is wrong. You can earn what you are worth and what the market will support (laws and fee caps excluded!).

Let's Look at the Numbers

A typical public adjusting company may use the following structure:

Total Claim Amount	% Company Fee	$ Company Fee	Claim Expenses	50% to Adjusters (After Expenses)	Net Company $ Profit	Net Company % Profit
$15,000	20%	$3,000	$0	$1,500	$1,500	50.0%
$15,000	20%	$3,000	$150	$1,425	$1,425	47.5%
$15,000	20%	$3,000	$500	$1,250	$1,250	41.7%
$75,000	20%	$15,000	$0	$7,500	$7,500	50.0%
$75,000	20%	$15,000	$150	$7,425	$7,425	49.5%
$75,000	20%	$15,000	$500	$7,250	$7,250	48.3%
$1,275,000	10%	$127,500	$6,750	$60,375	$60,375	47.4%
$1,275,000	20%	$255,000	$6,750	$124,125	$124,125	48.7%

Here you can see the variance of adjuster commission and company net profitability due to expenses. There are many instances where extraneous expenses such as industrial hygienists, weather forensic reports, roof drone imaging, etc. are taken out of the policyholders' monies.

Next, we recommend that you pull a percentage amount out of every claim fee you bring in to cover general office costs such as staff, rent, mailings, etc.

Total Claim Amount	% Company Fee	$ Company Fee	Claim Expenses	10% Office Fee	50% to Adjusters (After Expenses)	Net Company $ Profit	Net Company % Profit
$15,000	20%	$3,000	$0	$300	$1,350	$1,650	55.0%
$15,000	20%	$3,000	$150	$300	$1,275	$1,725	57.5%
$15,000	20%	$3,000	$500	$300	$1,100	$1,900	63.3%
$75,000	20%	$15,000	$0	$1,500	$6,750	$8,250	55.0%
$75,000	20%	$15,000	$150	$1,500	$6,675	$8,325	55.5%
$75,000	20%	$15,000	$500	$1,500	$6,500	$8,500	56.7%
$1,275,000	10%	$127,500	$6,750	$12,750	$54,000	$73,500	57.6%
$1,275,000	20%	$255,000	$6,750	$25,500	$111,375	$143,625	56.3%

If you don't have apprentices in your business (as of this writing, they are only legally required in Florida and California) plenty of public adjusting companies bring on junior adjusters for a training period. Their fees should either be a flat fee per claim or a small percentage to compensate for their time. Understand that you are giving them additional value in the form of education.

Total Claim Amount	% Company Fee	$ Company Fee	Claim Expenses	10% Office Fee	10% to Apprentice	50% to Adjusters (After Expenses)	Net Company $ Profit	Net Company % Profit
$15,000	20%	$3,000	$0	$300	$30	$1,335	$1,635	54.5%
$15,000	20%	$3,000	$150	$300	$30	$1,260	$1,560	52.0%
$15,000	20%	$3,000	$500	$300	$30	$1,085	$1,385	46.2%
$75,000	20%	$15,000	$0	$1,500	$150	$6,675	$8,175	54.5%
$75,000	20%	$15,000	$150	$1,500	$150	$6,600	$8,100	54.0%
$75,000	20%	$15,000	$500	$1,500	$150	$6,425	$7,925	52.8%
$1,275,000	10%	$127,500	$6,750	$12,750	$1,275	$53,363	$66,113	51.9%
$1,275,000	20%	$255,000	$6,750	$25,500	$2,550	$110,100	$135,600	53.2%

Be mindful that if you assign more than one public adjuster to a claim, you will need to carve up the 50% allotment — NOT give each adjuster 50%. In that case you are actually LOSING money!

A NOTE ON ROOFING SALES STRUCTURE

While public adjusting companies seem to have more commission structures than there are actual public adjusters in the world, roofing companies have a common formula. Since a good number of public adjusters come from the roofing world, it is worth putting in a fee comparison.

A typical payment structure in the insurance roofing world is 10/50/50. Breaking this down it represents:

- 10% off the top of the roof price to be used for overhead
- 50% after expenses to the roofing salesperson
- 50% after expenses to the roofing company (net profits)

While roofing companies typically calculate commissions using 10/50/50, it is important to know that sales representatives are paid 0% base. The more a salesperson wants to make, the more roofs they need to sell.

While it can be argued that 10% overhead is much too high for low hanging fruit during catastrophic events, overhead money is typically pooled together to pay for:

- Marketing
- Company trucks and fuel
- Staff training
- Leadership development
- Bonuses

The strategies and frameworks outlined in this chapter will serve as your compass, helping you navigate the complex landscape of public adjusting while building a sustainable and profitable enterprise. In the chapters that follow, we'll explore specific operational aspects of running a successful public adjusting business, beginning with essential marketing and client acquisition strategies.

RICH'S STORY

DEVELOPING & IMPLEMENTING A BUSINESS PLAN

Rich's experience working for another public adjusting company proved to be a valuable steppingstone in his career. While he admired the company's commitment to policyholders, Rich felt there was room for improvement in how claims were handled and how clients were served. This realization sparked his entrepreneurial spirit and set him on the path to developing his own unique approach to public adjusting.

During his time with the company, Rich observed both the strengths and weaknesses of their business model. He appreciated their dedication to clients but noticed inefficiencies in their processes and gaps in their service offerings. Rich began to envision a more streamlined, client-centric approach that could revolutionize the industry.

Driven by his desire to make a bigger impact, Rich started crafting his own business plan. He spent evenings and weekends researching market trends, analyzing competitor strategies, and identifying underserved niches in the public adjusting field. Rich's plan focused on leveraging technology to enhance claim processing efficiency, providing more personalized client communication, and offering additional support services to guide policyholders through the entire recovery process.

Rich's business plan also emphasized building a team of experts from diverse backgrounds, believing that a multidisciplinary approach would lead to more comprehensive claim assessments. He outlined strategies for marketing his services, managing finances, and scaling the business over time.

As Rich refined his plan, he became increasingly excited about the potential to create a public adjusting firm that truly put policyholders first. He envisioned a company that not only helped clients navigate the complexities of insurance claims but also educated them about their rights and empowered them throughout the process.

With his business plan complete, Rich felt confident in his vision and ready to take the leap into entrepreneurship. He knew the road ahead would be challenging, but he was determined to build a public adjusting firm that would set new standards in the industry.

CHAPTER 4
CONDUCTING MARKET RESEARCH

> The aim of marketing is to know and understand the customer so well the product or service fits him and sells itself.
>
> PETER DRUCKER

MARKET RESEARCH IS the compass that guides your public adjusting business toward success. It's the process of gathering and analyzing information about your target market, industry, and competition to make informed decisions and develop effective strategies. Here we will explore the crucial steps involved in conducting market research, starting with understanding your target market and analyzing the industry landscape.

The ideal target audience for a public adjusting business is primarily homeowners and commercial property owners who have recently experienced property damage. These individuals are often overwhelmed by the insurance claim process and are seeking expert assistance to get a fair settlement.

Demographics

Begin by defining the demographic characteristics of your target audience. For public insurance adjusting, you might find that homeowners, property managers, or business owners are key demographics to consider.

Psychographics

Psychographics delve into the psychological aspects of your audience. What are their values, interests, hobbies, and lifestyle choices? It is easy to fall into the trap that anyone with a damaged property and decent insurance coverage is a potential client, understanding psychographics can help you craft messages that resonate with your audience on a deeper level. For example, are they looking to rebuild a family home after a fire or restore real estate value on an investment property?

Challenges and Pain Points

Identify the challenges and pain points your target audience experiences when dealing with insurance claims. These could include delays in claim processing, disputes with insurance companies, or difficulties in assessing damages accurately.

Communication Preferences

Determine how your target audience prefers to receive information. Are they active on social media? Are they receptive to physical, printed mailers? Do they live in their email inbox? Understanding their communication preferences ensures that you can effectively reach and engage with them.

Behavioral Insights

Explore the behavioral patterns of your target audience. Are they proactive in seeking insurance assistance, or do they typically wait until they have been underpaid by the insurance company? Understanding their behavior can help you tailor your services to meet their expectations.

To succeed in the public adjusting industry, it's essential to know your ideal target audience. These are the individuals and businesses most likely to benefit from your services and become your clients. Identifying your target audience allows you to tailor your marketing efforts, service offerings, and communication to meet their specific needs.

- **Homeowners**

Often unfamiliar with the intricacies of insurance claims, they are more likely to seek expert help.

- **Commercial Property Owners**

They have more at stake financially and will look for specialized services to protect their investments.

- **Victims of Natural Disasters**

These are people who have recently experienced events like hurricanes, floods, or fires and urgently need to settle insurance claims.

- **Referral Partners**

Legal professionals, contractors, and real estate agents can also be part of your target audience as they can refer clients to you.

ANALYZE CUSTOMER PREFERENCES AND DEMOGRAPHICS

Market research goes beyond identifying your target audience; it also involves analyzing broader customer preferences and demographics. This deeper understanding helps you stay attuned to changes in the market and allows you to adapt your strategies accordingly.

Customer Preferences

Conduct surveys and interviews to gather insights into customer preferences. What do policyholders value most when seeking the services of a public adjuster? Is it quick response times, transparency in the claims process, or expertise in a specific type of claim? This doesn't need to be a formal survey but rather a casual conversation with prospective and existing clients.

Demographic Shifts

Keep an eye on demographic shifts that may impact your

target market. For instance, changes in the local population, such as an influx of retirees or young families, can influence the demand for certain types of insurance claims services.

Technology Adoption

Monitor how technology is influencing customer behavior and expectations. In today's digital age, policyholders may expect streamlined online claim submission processes or digital tools for assessing damages.

Competitive Analysis

Look at what your competitors are doing. Analyze their marketing strategies, service offerings, and customer feedback in online reviews. This analysis can provide insights into gaps in the market that your business can fill.

Understanding your target market is not just a one-time task; it's an ongoing process. The more accurately you can identify and understand your target audience, the better you can serve them, and the more successful your public adjusting business will be.

ASSESS MARKET TRENDS

In the realm of assessing market trends and opportunities in public adjusting, you should focus on several key aspects:

Emerging Trends

You need to be committed to being at the forefront of industry developments. Actively seek out and absorb information related to new trends, innovations, and strategies that can impact the world of public adjusting. This includes attending conferences, participating in industry forums, and engaging with thought leaders to gain valuable insights.

We would be doing you a disservice if we didn't stress that you follow and read Chip's blog, *Property Insurance Coverage Law Blog* to stay on the forefront of industry news.

Technological Advancements

Recognizing the pivotal role of technology in modern business, you need to pay special attention to technological advancements relevant to public adjusting. By embracing and integrating cutting-edge tools and software such as ClaimWizard, you ensure that your business remains competitive and efficient. Look to complementary industries such as roofing and restoration to incorporate technology tools such as drone imaging, measurement photography, and forensic weather reports to not only improve your standing against competition but increase your marketability and settlement amounts on claims.

Regulatory Updates

You need to be meticulous in tracking regulatory updates. In an industry where compliance is paramount, staying informed about changes in regulations and legal frameworks is crucial. This enables you to provide clients with accurate and reliable guidance while navigating the complexities of insurance claims. National, regional, and state industry organizations are a great place not just to stay up to date, but to network with peers and grow your business.

In essence, you need to adeptly navigate the intricate terrain of public adjusting, armed with a deep understanding of market trends, technological advancements, and regulatory intricacies. Your commitment to staying informed and adapting to change positions you as a proactive and influential figure within the industry.

HOW DO CHANGES IN MARKET TRENDS AFFECT PUBLIC ADJUSTING BUSINESSES?

Changes in market trends can have a significant impact on your public adjusting businesses. Businesses that specialize in helping policyholders navigate the insurance claims process and their success is closely tied to the dynamics of the insurance industry and the evolving needs of their clients. Here's how changes in market trends can affect public adjusting businesses.

Demand for Services

Market trends can influence the demand for public adjusting services. For example, during periods of increased natural disasters or large-scale insurance claims (such as hurricanes or wildfires), the demand for public adjusters may rise significantly. Conversely, during quieter periods, the demand may decrease. Public adjusting firms need to be prepared to scale their operations accordingly.

Technological Advancements

Advances in technology can streamline the claims process and change the way insurance companies handle claims. Public adjusters need to stay current with technology trends to ensure they can effectively represent their clients and navigate any new digital systems or tools implemented by insurance companies. Falling out of touch with improvements can leave you not only vulnerable to competition but lengthen your claim process time and reduce your efficiency — and profitability.

Regulatory Changes

Changes in insurance regulations and laws can impact how public adjusters operate. They must stay informed about these changes to ensure they remain compliant and can provide clients with accurate advice and assistance, otherwise they risk compliance issues that can affect their ability to work.

Market Competition

Market trends can also affect the competitive landscape. When there is increased demand for public adjusting services, more firms may enter the market. Public adjusting businesses need to differentiate themselves and offer unique value propositions to remain competitive.

Specialization

Public adjusting businesses may need to adapt by specializing in specific niches or types of claims, such as commercial property claims or homeowners' insurance. Specialization can help them stay competitive and meet the unique needs of clients in specific market segments such as municipalities, churches, and the hospitality industry.

Insurance Industry Practices

Changes in the way insurance companies write policies and handle claims can impact the strategies and tactics that public adjusters employ to maximize settlements for their clients.

Public adjusting businesses must stay agile and adaptable to respond effectively to changes in market trends. Being proactive, staying informed, and continuously evolving their strategies and services are essential for these businesses to thrive in a dynamic and competitive industry.

ANALYZE THE COMPETITION

Competition in the public adjusting field can be fierce, but there are always gaps in the market that can be exploited. Specializing in a particular type of claim, offering additional services, or even focusing on niche policyholder communities can set you apart. Analyzing the competition is a critical aspect of market research. It allows you to understand who you're up against and how you can differentiate your public adjusting business. Simultaneously, it can reveal untapped market opportunities that you can leverage to your advantage.

Competitor Landscape

Create a comprehensive list of your competitors in the public adjusting field. This includes both local and national firms. Understand their strengths, weaknesses, and areas of specialization. Here I would like to note that you shouldn't be overly concerned about what your competition is doing, but rather use it as a way to find a differentiation for your own company and services. Unlike many other industries, your competition can quickly turn into allies when needed.

Service Offerings

Analyze the range of services your competitors offer. Do they focus on specific types of claims, such as fire damage or flood damage? Do they assist with releasing funds from mortgage companies? Do they utilize tools such as drone imaging? Assess whether there are unmet needs or underserved segments of the market.

Pricing Strategies

Examine the pricing strategies of your competitors. Are they positioned as premium service providers, or do they compete on affordability? Consider how your pricing strategy aligns with the value you offer.

Customer Reviews and Feedback

Review customer testimonials, online reviews, and feedback about your competitors. Pay attention to common pain points mentioned by clients. This can help you tailor your services to address these issues more effectively.

Market Gaps

Identify gaps or shortcomings in the services provided by your competitors. Are there areas where they consistently receive negative feedback or where they lack expertise? These gaps represent opportunities for your business to excel. (Teaser: Lack of frequent and transparent communication is often the most-cited complaint of policyholders.)

IDENTIFYING YOUR UNIQUE SELLING PROPOSITION

In an industry like public adjusting, it's essential to identify your Unique Selling Proposition (USP) and competitive advantages. Your USPs are the qualities or features that distinguish your business from competitors and make you stand out in the eyes of potential clients.

Consider what sets your public adjusting business apart. Is it your deep expertise in a specific type of claim, your outstanding customer service, or your innovative technology solutions? These are all potential USPs that can be highlighted in your business plan and marketing materials.

Once you've identified your USP, the next step is to articulate your value proposition – a concise statement that communicates the unique benefits and solutions your business offers to policyholders. Your value proposition should answer the question: "Why should a client choose your public insurance adjusting services over those of your competitors?"

A well-crafted value proposition is a powerful marketing tool that can attract clients and build trust. It should be prominently featured in your business plan and marketing materials. Here's an example of a value proposition for a public adjusting business:

> We empower policyholders by leveling the playing field in the insurance claims process. As advocates dedicated to securing maximum, fair settlements, we handle the complexities of claims so our clients can focus on rebuilding and recovery. Our expertise, transparency, and relentless commitment ensure every policyholder receives the full benefits they're entitled to under their policy.
>
> When disaster strikes, we stand in your corner—protecting your interests, reducing your stress, and delivering results that help you move forward with confidence.

Your value proposition should resonate with your target audience and convey the tangible benefits they will receive by choosing your services. It's the promise you make to your clients, and delivering on that promise is key to building lasting relationships and a strong reputation in the industry.

Understanding the importance of a business plan is essential for the success and growth of public adjusting businesses, whether they are startups or well-established enterprises.

Business plans provide clarity of purpose, guide strategic decision-making, and serve as a communication tool for stakeholders. They are living documents that should be regularly updated to remain relevant and effective.

Defining your mission, vision, and goals sets the direction for your business and reinforces its identity and values. Crafting a compelling mission statement and setting ambitious yet realistic goals are essential steps in this process.

Additionally, identifying your Unique Selling Points and competitive advantages and articulating clear value are crucial for attracting clients and differentiating your business from competitors. Your value proposition is the promise you make to policyholders, and delivering on that promise is key to building trust and credibility in the public insurance adjusting industry.

When looking at ways to develop goals and expected outcomes for your public adjusting or first-party claims business, incorporate a SWOT analysis framework.

Business advisors often use SWOT analysis which represents Strengths, Weaknesses, Opportunities, and Threats.

Strengths

Understand that by outlining and being specific about your strengths, you will be able to develop and identify what elements of the company are worthwhile and point to each of those elements with good definitions.

Weaknesses

If you first decipher your weaknesses, you can predict measurable outcomes. The goal here is to minimize or eliminate any weaknesses after measuring how they will affect your company.

Opportunities

Success lies in identifying growth areas and capitalizing on competitive advantages. Expanding into underserved markets, utilizing advanced technology, and building strategic partnerships create opportunities to enhance market share and service offerings. Proactively addressing industry trends and customer needs ensures sustainable growth and positions the company as a leader in the field.

Threats

Often, if you define threats upfront, you can use these threats realistically and define or change them to enhance the project to the realistic positive outcome you want.

SWOT MATRIX

Review your SWOT. These items should be accounted for on your matrix. Just because you should be working on an area for your company to move forward right now, you should still be documenting and planning for the others. By working this way, you are not only helping your business now but planning for the future.

Below are some examples of SWOT analysis responses specific to the public adjusting industry. Each quadrant contains possible points; ONE company wouldn't have all these items at the same time.

Strengths	Weaknesses
• Company has repeat clients • Company has strong customer service • Company has great client, carrier, and vendor relationships • Clients give positive word-of-mouth and recommend your company over others • Strong lead funnel and sales presentation results and high rate of signed contracts • Adjusters and sales representatives are free of administrative tasks so they can focus on signing more claims and adjusting/settling more claims faster • Office staff have clearly defined roles that are easy to assign, track, and delegate	• Communication is time consuming between clients/staff & staff/staff • Missed deadlines • Overdue or forgotten tasks • Sloppy documentation that is difficult to recall when needed • High percentage of lost/unsigned clients • Not being tech savvy • Scattered communication across email, phone, text, and in-person • Inconsistent decisions across company and team • Not able to effectively deal with daily claims when a catastrophic event comes in
Opportunities	**Threats**
• Front office person is a wiz at in-person events and would be amazing at home shows and networking events • We've never taken the time to go back for recoverable deprecation on large loss claims • We haven't brought in any Apprentices to our company • Our webpage ranks very high in SERPs without much work on our part, but we don't know if we are getting leads from it • New adjuster has a roofing background and lots of contacts in that industry • We are the only Public Adjusting company in the area with staff licensed to operate drones commercially	• Potential clients are calling other PAs because our initial response is too slow • Signed clients are cancelling contracts because of lack of communication • Fee collection takes too long and/or many unpaid client invoices • Have to pass up on claims because we can't handle the additional workload • Documentation taking too long to generate or formalize • Spend too much time in any one area of work/claims • Hold on to claims longer than we should before passing to an attorney

TOWS ANALYSIS

Next, you will want to take your SWOT analysis and create actionable items. What good is knowing your strengths if you aren't going to use them or your weaknesses if you aren't fixing them? The TOWS (Threats, Opportunities, Weaknesses, and Strengths — SWOT in reverse) matrix gives you the matching tactic to address your strong/weak points.

	Opportunities **External / Positive**	Threats **External / Negative**
Strengths **Internal / Positive**	Strength - Opportunity **Strategies:** Which of your strengths can be used to maximize the opportunities you identified?	Strength - Threats **Strategies:** How can you use your strengths to minimize the threats you identified?
Weaknesses **Internal / Negative**	Weakness - Opportunity **Strategies:** What action(s) can you take to minimize your weaknesses using the opportunities you identified?	Weakness - Threats **Strategies:** How can you minimize or eliminate your weaknesses to avoid the threats you identified?

SWOT/TOWS ANALYSIS

When you're finished with the SWOT and TOWS analysis, you'll have an insightful look at your company, accompanied by a list of strategies that you can implement to better your business.

Take this list of strategies and start implementing them. If some designs are long-term plans, break them into steps with specific milestones and put each one on your calendar so you can implement the change over time.

Now that you have this business resource, you'll want to keep it handy. Hang it on your office wall or keep it on your desktop to reference it throughout the year as you make decisions. Your hard work will pay off.

Aside from strategic plans, here are additional benefits from your completed SWOT / TOWS analysis.

- Improved Focus — This analysis should put everyone on the same page. It identifies what you should be working toward this year.
- Strategic Alignment — Owners and team members can build better strategies together with everyone working on the same goals.
- Identify Unknown Aspects — You'll likely discover parts of your business that you didn't know about.

Uncovering this information will help you move forward from unknown strengths to hidden threats.

If you are one of the many business owners who set aside time to finish each step of your SWOT analysis, we'd like to congratulate you. You have made great strides toward improving your public adjusting business!

RICH'S STORY

CONDUCTING MARKET RESEARCH

As Rich delved into research for his new public adjusting business, he quickly realized that running a company was vastly different from handling claims. His expertise in claim adjustment was undeniable, but the intricacies of business ownership presented a new set of challenges he hadn't anticipated.

Rich found himself grappling with questions he'd never considered before. Who exactly was his target audience? How could he differentiate his services from established competitors? What were the current trends shaping the industry? These questions led him down a path of intensive research and self-reflection.

He spent countless hours poring over industry reports, analyzing competitor strategies, and studying market trends. Rich conducted surveys and interviews with potential clients, seeking to understand their pain points and needs. He was surprised to discover that many policyholders were unaware of the benefits a public adjuster could provide, highlighting a significant opportunity for education and outreach.

As he compiled his findings, Rich struggled to translate this wealth of information into actionable strategies. He realized that his skills in claim assessment didn't necessarily equip him for tasks like marketing, financial planning, and business development. This revelation was humbling but also motivating.

Determined to overcome these challenges, Rich sought advice from mentors in the business world and enrolled in several online courses on entrepreneurship and marketing. He learned to conduct SWOT analyses, develop customer personas, and create targeted marketing campaigns.

Through this process, Rich gained a deeper appreciation for the complexities of running a business. He understood that success wouldn't just come from his ability to handle claims effectively, but also from his capacity to attract clients, manage resources, and adapt to market demands. This realization, though daunting, reinforced Rich's commitment to building a public adjusting firm that would not only serve clients well but also thrive as a business entity.

CHAPTER 5
BUILDING A PROFESSIONAL NETWORK

> Networking is not about just connecting people. It's about connecting people with people, people with ideas, and people with opportunities.
>
> MICHELE JENNAE

SUCCESSFUL PUBLIC INSURANCE adjusting requires the creation, nurturing, and expansion of a professional and business network which is the lifeblood of enduring success. This chapter explores the art of building a robust professional network. Successful networking is a journey that intertwines the dual pillars of establishing strong, lasting relationships with policyholder clients and forging effective collaborations with other industry professionals so that the public adjuster or the business is top of mind whenever a need for claims services arises.

The cornerstone of a thriving public adjuster's practice lies in the depth and quality of its relationships. These relationships, cultivated with both policyholders and ancillary providers of service to policyholder clients, form a dynamic ecosystem where trust, expertise, and mutual benefit converge. Strategic networking is not just about expanding business opportunities; it's about creating a self-sustaining cycle of growth and reputation.

A significant milestone for any public adjuster is reaching the point where their business becomes predominantly fueled by repeat and referral business. This is not an overnight achievement but the result of consistent, quality interactions and the establishment of a reputation for excellence. When policyholders return for services and confidently refer others, it signifies a level of trust and satisfaction that is the gold standard in any service industry. Similarly, when other servicers of policyholder needs, such as attorneys, contractors, inspectors, and fellow adjusters, become sources of referrals, it reflects a recognition of expertise and reliability.

This chapter guides you through the nuances of building such a network. We explore how to lay the foundational stones of trust with policyholders, ensuring each interaction adds to a reservoir of goodwill and professional respect. We also navigate the intricacies of collaborating with other professionals, understanding each relationship within the industry is a thread in a larger web of mutual support and growth. From the initial handshake or introductory email to the complex interactions of claim negotiations and collaborative problem-solving, every touchpoint is an opportunity to reinforce and expand your network.

The digital age has transformed how professionals connect and maintain relationships, offering new avenues and challenges in building a network which not only spans geographies but also bridges various aspects of the insurance and property industries.

This chapter is not just about the mechanics of networking; it's about cultivating a mindset where every interaction is seen as a step towards building a sustainable, referral-driven business. It's about understanding that in the world of public insurance adjusting, your network is your net worth, and the strength of your relationships is the measure of your success.

BUILD PARTNERSHIPS

Public adjusting is a business that thrives on relationships. A little goodwill now can yield profitable, long-term clients later. Here we'll take a look at each of these groups and examine the ways your public claims adjusting business can become indispensable to them.

- Retail Establishment — home improvement stores, plumbing supply shops, flooring warehouses
- Professional Service Providers — architects, interior designers, commercial and residential real estate agents, mortgage companies
- Industry-Related Companies — roofers, temporary housing providers, restoration companies, dry-out companies, pack-out companies, property management firms

Come up with what you would offer their existing clientele. For example, by partnering with a plumbing supply shop, you may be able to help clients who are having a hard time replacing the damaged property with like-kind quality and price fixtures. Partnering with an interior designer may be helpful when a client is attempting to maximize their claim payout to cover rebuilding the damaged property. Cultivating a relationship with your area's top roofing companies is a no-brainer. Design marketing and create the materials that partners can easily hand to their clients and make your public adjusting services known.

In reciprocation, recommend these business partnership

connections to your clients as they are remediating or rebuilding their damaged property. When under the stress of a property loss, there is rarely a better recommendation than a vendor that will show up when they say they will and complete a great job on time for the price quoted. YOU should be the person to give your client that recommendation.

Build and Nurture Vendor Relationships

Strong business relationships often occur when both parties can offer value. Instead of only looking at how your vendors can help you, consider the value that you provide to them. In some cases, simply listening and offering business advice is the value you add to the relationship. An opportunity for value is to provide new contacts or potential customers with a vendor. Put yourself in the place of your business contacts to determine what type of benefits they may hope to receive from you.

Contact Regularly

If you only call on your business contacts when you need something from them, they will likely feel used and unappreciated. Touch base with your peers and vendors regularly. This keeps you updated on their activities and business projects while building a relationship with them. Take an interest beyond the business aspect by getting to know more about their personal lives. When you get to know one another better, you are better able to partner up on business pursuits. A great tactic is the 'scroll and dial' where you open your phone address book, randomly scroll your contacts, and choose five EVERY DAY to contact. *Just because.*

Build Trust

Trust and honesty fuel a positive relationship in the business world. If you fail to interact honestly with your contacts, you develop a sense of mistrust that may cause vendors and colleagues to be guarded around you. In some cases, honesty means admitting that you don't know an answer or made a mistake. Showing this side of yourself sends the message that you are genuine and honest.

Keep Your Options Open

It can be tempting to put all your eggs in one basket regarding utilizing vendors. It makes it seem like operations work smoothly, and everyone is getting business. Keep in mind that your business and your customers are the most important.

You might want to allow yourself room to grow. Competitive offers can come daily. Just because you've been partnered with a vendor for years, it doesn't mean you're getting a bigger slice of their time and attention.

You always want to study what others have to offer. Better prices for you generally mean better rates for your customers, which will make them come back more often. Be warned, that quality trumps price every time.

Ask for Expert Opinions

Before you contemplate running your business with an iron fist, consider this. Vendors don't just give you a random price for their services. They can bring so much more value and knowledge to the partnership.

Since you're dealing with other small business owners, remember that they are the experts on the topic and not you. Involving them when you want to develop new marketing strategies or service offerings can benefit both parties greatly.

COLLABORATE WITH INDUSTRY PROFESSIONALS

Teaming up with industry pros is key to success. Think of it as forming a supergroup, where attorneys, contractors, and fellow adjusters bring their A-game to help policyholders get the settlements they deserve. It's not just about working together; it's about combining expertise to offer top-notch service. Whether it's getting insights from legal eagles, details from savvy contractors, or wisdom from experienced adjusters, collaboration boosts your ability to deliver. After all, navigating insurance claims is a team sport, and by joining forces, you're not just doing a job; you're ensuring justice for policyholders. In public adjusting, working with other pros isn't just smart; it's the secret sauce to making a real difference.

Collaborations with other industry pros not only broadens the scope of services you can offer to policyholders, it also creates avenues for mutual referrals and shared expertise. Let's expand on the roles of some key professionals and how they can collaborate with public adjusters.

General Contractors and Roofing Companies

Much of the work that building, roof, plumbing, and electrical contractors get is to rebuild property damage, a good portion of which may be covered by an insurance claim. Building relationships with these contractors is a great way to grow your business. By offering a free inspection for projects they are working on, you can discover claims that will offset the inspection cost and help put your claims adjusting company first on their go-to list.

Also, policyholders frequently contact contractors to fix property damage when they could use a public claims adjuster to negotiate a better settlement for the damage. Working with contractors can help you identify those situations where a policyholder may be unaware of the benefits you could provide.

- Collaboration Opportunities: Public adjusters can collaborate with contractors to obtain accurate repair estimates, validate the scope of work, and ensure quality repairs. This collaboration is vital for preparing a precise and fair claim settlement.
- Joint Assessments and Solutions: Contractors can provide detailed insights into the extent of damage and the necessary repairs, which can be invaluable in substantiating a claim. Public adjusters, in turn, can

assist contractors in understanding the insurance aspect, ensuring their services align with the policyholder's coverage.

Restoration Companies

Many property owners choose to restore rather than rebuild — mainly if the property contains classic (and expensive) architectural features like Victorian turrets or historic stained glass. Architectural restorers frequently uncover hidden damage during the course of their work. By contacting restorers and offering a free inspection of projects they are working on, you may unveil claims covered by the owner's policy that warrants filing a claim.

Real Estate and Insurance Attorneys

Real estate attorneys encompass a wealth of experience and documentation about the properties in your area. They also administrate the contracts between homeowners associations (HOAs) and property owners. So they are familiar with the types of damage claims and which properties are most vulnerable. Uncovering a claim can reduce their headaches and put money in your pocket.

Attorneys specializing in insurance law are crucial allies in navigating the legal complexities that may arise during the claims process. Attorneys who are counsel for policyholders who have suffered a loss often need assistance from public adjusters and may refer their clients for help.

- Collaboration Opportunities: Public adjusters can work closely with attorneys to address legal challenges in claim disputes, especially with valuation and appraisal opportunities. Attorneys often need the expertise of a qualified public adjuster to present a claim.

- Referral and Support Network: Attorneys can refer clients to public adjusters when they identify a need for specialized claim handling expertise. Public adjusters should never practice law and should therefore establish relationships where they can obtain legal coverage opinions from attorneys well-versed in property insurance law.

HOAS and Property Mangers/Investors

Real estate investors hate paying out of pocket for property repairs. So, if you're willing to take the time to do a quick free property inspection, any claim you find is more business for you and money the investor can use to repair the property. Another good source of business leads is homeowners associations (HOAs) and property managers. Offering to provide a brief on-site presentation about the benefits of your claims adjustment services can mean big business for you the next time fire, flood, or other damage strikes.

Identify the HOAs in your area and properties where you're most likely to find claims. Some properties may be more prone to flood damage or erosion, others to fallen trees or roof wear, and others to paving issues. Identifying potential claim areas can help you understand a potential client's needs.

Meet with property investors and managers in your area. Those with multiple properties may prefer to work with a single adjuster whom they can trust. It simplifies their business and puts more money in your pocket.

Property managers play a crucial role in managing and maintaining properties, especially in the aftermath of a loss. They are often among the first to identify and assess property damage and can be instrumental in initiating the claims process.

- Collaboration Opportunities: Public adjusters can collaborate with property managers to provide timely

assessments and claims assistance for managed properties. This partnership ensures property managers can swiftly address their tenants' needs while adjusters can offer their expertise right at the onset of a claim.
- Mutual Referrals: Property managers can refer public adjusters to their clients experiencing property loss, while public adjusters can recommend property managers to policyholders needing professional property management services post-restoration.

Risk Managers

Risk managers specialize in identifying, assessing, and mitigating risks associated with property and business operations. They are key figures in preparing for and responding to losses.

- Collaboration Opportunities: Public adjusters can work with risk managers to develop comprehensive claims strategies that align with the policyholder's risk management plans. This collaboration ensures a more holistic approach to claim resolution and risk mitigation.
- Expertise Sharing: Risk managers can provide valuable insights into risk assessment and mitigation strategies, which can be beneficial for public adjusters in understanding the broader context of a claim.

Insurance Agents

Insurance agents are often the primary point of contact for policyholders when purchasing insurance policies and can play a supportive role during the claims process.

- Collaboration Opportunities: Public adjusters can collaborate with insurance agents to ensure policyholders receive the full benefits of their insurance coverage. This partnership can help in clarifying policy terms and coverage limits, leading to more effective claim handling.
- Referral Network: Insurance agents can refer policyholders to public adjusters when they identify a complex claim situation that may benefit from specialized expertise. In turn, public adjusters can refer clients to insurance agents for policy renewals or adjustments.

Accountants

Accountants, especially those specializing in forensic accounting, can be crucial in quantifying financial losses, particularly in complex business interruption claims.

- Collaboration Opportunities: Public adjusters can work with accountants to accurately assess financial losses and present a detailed claim to the insurer. This collaboration is particularly valuable in business interruption claims where the financial intricacies can be quite complex.
- Complementary Expertise: Accountants can offer detailed financial analysis and documentation that can bolster a claim's accuracy, while public adjusters can provide the necessary insurance knowledge to ensure the claim is filed correctly and comprehensively.

Experts – Engineers and Architects

Both engineers and architects work closely with contractors and property owners on rebuilding or repair projects.

- Collaboration Opportunities: Public adjusters not only use the expertise of the engineer or architect, but these experts can also be a great source if they determine the need for a public adjuster. This collaboration could be mutually beneficial for the engineer or architect, as the project could evolve into additional work for them.
- Joint Assessments and Solutions: On larger or more sophisticated claims, a public adjuster often needs the services of these experts to prove the damages. In return, these same experts may refer a public adjuster for a customer of their own.

Appraisers

Appraisers, contractors, and specialized estimators have knowledge about valuing property and damages. All estimating platforms call for obtaining local pricing for verification. Building relationships with them ensures accurate and fair valuation in claims, which is crucial for policyholder satisfaction and claim resolution. Specialty items and construction often need experts to provide information for accurate claim valuation.

Peers - Other Public Adjusters

In some cases, another public adjuster might lack the manpower, expertise, or financial resources to handle a claim. Another situation is where one public adjuster receives a lead where a policyholder is in need of a public adjuster, but it is not in their area. Networking with fellow public adjusters can lead to knowledge sharing, mentorship opportunities, and collaboration in handling large or complex claims. It can also provide a support system for case overflow or specialized expertise in certain types of claims.

- Collaboration Opportunities: It is not uncommon for

one public adjuster to bring another public adjuster on to a claim to help or even take the claim over.

- Joint Assessment and Solutions: A public adjuster working with another public adjuster allows both public adjusters to combine their strengths and cover the other's weaknesses. Networking with other public adjusters from other areas can allow each to refer leads and receive leads, thus expanding their collaborative network.

In summary, collaborating with contractors, attorneys, property managers, risk managers, insurance agents, accountants, experts like engineers and architects, appraisers, and other public adjusters can significantly enhance a public adjuster's ability to serve policyholders effectively. These collaborations not only lead to mutual benefits and shared expertise but also open up opportunities for referrals, thereby expanding the network and reach of a public adjuster's practice. By understanding and leveraging the roles of these professionals, public adjusters can offer more comprehensive solutions to policyholders and establish themselves as integral parts of a collaborative network in the aftermath of a loss.

RICH'S STORY

BUILDING A PROFESSIONAL NETWORK

Rich discovered that building a professional network was a crucial aspect of his public adjusting business. While initially daunting, he soon found ways to integrate networking into his daily routine, striking a balance between working on claims and fostering valuable connections.

He began attending industry conferences and local business meetups, viewing them as opportunities to learn and share experiences rather than mere obligations. Rich joined professional associations, finding that these memberships provided not only networking opportunities but also valuable resources and educational content that enhanced his expertise.

Rich invested time in building relationships with contractors, attorneys, and other professionals who could potentially refer clients to him. He scheduled occasional coffee meetings and lunch dates, approaching these interactions as chances to build genuine relationships rather than purely business transactions. To his surprise, he found himself enjoying these connections, realizing they offered fresh perspectives on the industry.

Social media became an unexpected ally in his networking efforts. Rich established a routine of spending a short time each day on platforms like LinkedIn, sharing insights and engaging with others in the field. He found that this consistent, manageable approach yielded better results than sporadic, intensive efforts.

As his network grew, Rich noticed an increase in referrals and a growing reputation in the industry. He realized that networking, while sometimes challenging to balance with his claim work, was an integral part of building and sustaining his business. It wasn't just about finding new clients; it was about creating a support system within the industry.

Rich came to appreciate that networking didn't have to feel like a separate full-time job. Instead, it became a natural extension of his passion for public adjusting, allowing him to connect with like-minded professionals and ultimately serve his clients better.

CHAPTER 6
TECHNOLOGY AND TOOLS FOR EFFICIENCY

Technology is best when it brings people together.

MATT MULLENWEG

IN THE REALM of any business — especially public adjusting — efficiency and accuracy are supreme. ClaimWizard emerges as a beacon of technomancy, offering a suite of features designed to enhance the claim-handling process. Its powerful platform not only streamlines operations but also provides specialized tools tailored for public adjusting.

The ClaimWizard platform stands out for its ability to manage complex claim processes, offering an integrated solution that simplifies the handling of a wide range of claims. With its intuitive interface and robust functionality, users can easily navigate through claims, ensuring a more efficient and accurate process. This efficiency translates into faster claim resolutions, increased client satisfaction, and a noticeable improvement in operational productivity.

In the interest of full disclosure, as a co-founder of ClaimWizard, I acknowledge my bias. However, the platform's position as the industry's leading claims management software is demonstrated by its widespread adoption over the past 12 years among successful public adjusting firms. It has a proven track record of streamlining operations, improving compliance, and increasing settlement values for nearly one million property insurance claims across five countries.

LYNETTE

IMPLEMENTING CLAIMWIZARD IN YOUR BUSINESS

Incorporating ClaimWizard into your business operations requires a strategic approach. The first step involves assessing how ClaimWizard aligns with your specific business needs. This assessment includes understanding the volume and complexity of claims your business handles, and how ClaimWizard's features can cater to these requirements.

Once the decision to implement ClaimWizard is made, planning the integration process is crucial. This involves setting realistic expectations regarding the timeline and potential challenges during the transition. Effective planning also includes training staff and ensuring they are comfortable with the new system.

Collaboration with the ClaimWizard team is instrumental for a smooth integration. Their expertise can guide you through the setup, customization, and troubleshooting processes, ensuring that the platform works seamlessly with your existing claim workflows.

Streamlining Claim Intake and Management

ClaimWizard revolutionizes the intake of new claims. Its streamlined process allows for quick and efficient claim entry, reducing the time spent on manual data entry. This system ensures that every claim is captured accurately and is readily accessible for further processing.

Centralizing claim information in a unified system is another cornerstone of ClaimWizard. This centralization means all relevant data, from client information to claim details, is stored in one place, making it easier for adjusters to access and manage claims. This feature significantly reduces the time spent searching for information, thus increasing overall productivity.

Automated workflows are perhaps the most significant feature of ClaimWizard in terms of improving efficiency. These workflows guide the claim through each stage of the process, ensuring that nothing is overlooked. Automation reduces the likelihood of human error and speeds up the claim handling process, allowing adjusters to focus on more complex tasks.

Automating Repetitive Tasks

Automation in public insurance adjusting is a game-changer, particularly when it comes to repetitive and time-consuming tasks. Identifying tasks that can be automated is the first step in this transformation. These often include data entry, claim status updates, and routine communication with clients.

Implementing software solutions to automate these tasks brings a multitude of benefits. It significantly reduces the time and effort spent on manual processes, allowing adjusters to focus on more complex and high-value aspects of their work. Furthermore, automation minimizes human error, ensuring more accurate and consistent outcomes in claim processing.

The overall impact of task automation on operational efficiency is profound. It streamlines workflows, speeds up claim processing, and enhances the accuracy of work, leading to increased productivity and client satisfaction.

Digitizing Claim Documentation and Processes

The transition from paper-based systems or disjointed online storage to a true automated digital workflow has marked a significant leap in operational efficiency. This digitization encompasses all aspects of claim handling, from documentation to process management.

Electronic signatures and document management systems are central to this digital transformation. These technologies not only expedite the documentation process but also enhance security and compliance with regulatory standards. By digitizing documents, adjusters can easily store, retrieve, and share important claim files, facilitating smoother and faster claim processing.

Streamlining claim processes through digital transformation results in more efficient and scalable operations. It enables adjusters to handle a larger volume of claims with greater precision, ultimately leading to a more robust and resilient business model.

Reporting and Analytics

In today's data-driven world, leveraging reporting and analytics tools is essential for informed decision-making in public insurance adjusting. These tools allow adjusters to analyze claim data to identify trends, patterns, and performance metrics. By understanding these metrics, adjusters can make more informed decisions, streamline their processes, and improve overall efficiency.

Utilizing insights from analytics also helps in optimizing business strategies. Adjusters can identify areas for improvement, develop better claim handling techniques, and even foresee potential challenges. This proactive approach, enabled by analytics, positions businesses to stay ahead in a competitive market.

Enhancing Customer Experience Through Technology

In the digital age, customer expectations are continually evolving. Implementing customer portals and mobile apps has become essential for businesses looking to enhance their customer experience. These technologies provide clients with easy access to claim information, updates, and communication tools.

By utilizing mobile apps and online platforms, adjusters can offer clients a seamless and convenient way to engage with their claims. This level of accessibility and transparency greatly improves client satisfaction and trust in the adjusting process.

A customer-centric approach in leveraging technology not only enhances the client experience but also strengthens the adjuster-client relationship. It positions the adjuster as a forward-thinking, client-focused professional, which is key to building long-term client loyalty in a competitive industry.

DOCUMENTATION AND COMMUNICATION TOOLS

Effective documentation and communication are the backbones of successful public insurance adjusting. Tools designed for capturing and organizing claim documentation streamline this aspect of claim management. These tools often include features for document storage, retrieval, and sharing, ensuring that all necessary paperwork is easily accessible.

Streamlining communication with clients, insurance carriers, and other stakeholders is another area where technology plays a crucial role. With the right tools, adjusters can maintain clear and constant communication channels, providing updates, sharing documents, and collaborating more effectively. This not only improves the efficiency of the claim process but also enhances the overall client experience.

The importance of clear and secure document management systems cannot be overstated. These systems protect sensitive client information and ensure compliance with industry regulations, safeguarding both the client and the adjuster.

CLAIM VALUATION AND ESTIMATION TOOLS

In the intricate world of public adjusting, the accuracy of claim valuation and estimation is critical. Advanced software solutions have been developed to assess damages and accurately value claims. These tools utilize data analytics and machine learning algorithms to provide adjusters with precise and reliable estimates for damages, repair costs, and replacement values.

The benefits of using such software are multifaceted. They not only enhance the accuracy of claim valuations, reducing the likelihood of disputes and rework, but also expedite the overall process. This increased efficiency leads to quicker claim resolutions and higher client satisfaction.

Exploring tools for estimating repair costs and replacement values, adjusters can access a wealth of information, including industry standards, local pricing data, and historical claims data. This information is invaluable in creating accurate and fair claim estimates, ensuring that clients are adequately compensated, and insurance companies are not overcharged.

In today's rapidly evolving insurance landscape, technology tools are no longer a luxury but a necessity for public adjusters. From automated workflows and digital documentation to analytics and customer portals, these solutions transform how claims are managed and valued. The return on investment extends beyond efficiency – leading to enhanced client satisfaction, improved accuracy, and increased claim capacity. As the industry advances, those who embrace these innovations will be best positioned to serve their clients effectively and build more profitable practices.

RICH'S STORY

TECHNOLOGY AND TOOLS FOR EFFICIENCY

Rich initially attempted to manage his public adjusting business using a combination of spreadsheets and various customer relationship management (CRM) tools. He spent hours meticulously updating claim statuses, tracking client interactions, and managing deadlines. While this system worked in the beginning, Rich soon found himself overwhelmed as his business grew. He realized that the time spent on administrative tasks was taking away from his ability to focus on serving his clients and growing his business. It only took one lost claim due to missing critical deadlines and documentation to realize he needed a better solution.

Frustrated with the inefficiencies of his cobbled-together system, Rich began researching more comprehensive solutions. That's when he discovered ClaimWizard, a specialized software designed specifically for public adjusters. Initially skeptical, Rich decided to give it a try.

From the moment he started using ClaimWizard, Rich was amazed at how much easier it made his workflow. The software had already anticipated the key elements he needed to track for each claim, from initial intake to final settlement. Rich found that tasks that once took hours now could be completed in minutes.

ClaimWizard's automated reminders ensured that no deadlines were missed, and its centralized document storage made accessing important files a breeze. The software's reporting features provided Rich with valuable insights into his business performance, allowing him to make data-driven decisions.

Perhaps most importantly, ClaimWizard freed up a significant amount of Rich's time. He no longer had to spend evenings updating spreadsheets or weekends organizing files. Instead, he could focus on what he did best: advocating for his clients and growing his business.

Rich realized that investing in the right technology was not just about efficiency; it was about giving himself the freedom to be the best public adjuster he could be. With ClaimWizard handling the administrative heavy lifting, Rich felt more confident than ever in his ability to scale his business while maintaining the high level of service his clients deserved.

PART THREE
ADVANCED BUSINESS STRATEGIES

CHAPTER 7
MARKETING AND BRANDING STRATEGIES

> Your brand is what other people say about you when you're not in the room.
>
> JEFF BEZOS

LET'S get straight to the point: the effort you've poured into your business plan is about to show its true value. By now, you should have already tackled the essentials: crafting your company's mission and value statements, pinpointing your target audience, carving out your unique selling proposition, and conducting a thorough SWOT analysis.

DEFINE YOUR BRAND IDENTITY

Now, we're diving into a crucial, game-changing phase for your public adjusting company: designing brand elements. This is the foundation for building a robust, instantly recognizable brand identity. So, let's roll up our sleeves and delve into how exactly you can master this for a business that's all about public adjusting. Brand identity includes your company logo, but also includes making good decisions about the color scheme, typography, imagery, and graphics you'll use in your marketing materials.

Logo

When designing a logo for a public adjusting company, several key elements need to be considered to ensure it effectively represents the brand's core values of trust, protection, and resilience. The logo should incorporate symbols that evoke these qualities, such as shields, roofs, or abstract figures that symbolize support and guidance. A balance between simplicity and distinctiveness is crucial; the logo should be straightforward enough to be memorable yet unique enough to stand out. It's important to avoid overly complex designs that might not be versatile across various mediums, particularly when the logo is scaled down for smaller items.

Ensuring the logo's consistency across different mediums — whether printed, embroidered, or screen-printed — is essential. This might mean simplifying certain design elements to ensure they are effective in all formats. In the digital realm, the logo should be optimized for use on websites, social media, and digital ads, taking into account how it appears on screens of varying sizes and resolutions.

Finally, once the logo design is finalized, legal protection through trademarking is an important step to safeguard the brand identity. This comprehensive approach to logo design ensures that the logo not only resonates with the brand's values but is also versatile and effective across a wide range of applications.

Color Scheme

When it comes to the color scheme for public adjusters, understanding the psychology of color is crucial, as different hues can evoke a range of emotions. It's vital to select colors that embody stability, trust, and confidence, aligning with the nature of the public adjusting profession.

Blues are typically linked with trust and dependability, making them an excellent choice for conveying a sense of reliability. Greens, on the other hand, are associated with growth and renewal, which can also resonate well in this context. Moreover, maintaining consistency in the chosen color palette across all marketing and branding materials is key. This uniformity not only aids in establishing brand recognition but also projects a professional image, crucial for building trust with clients and stakeholders in the field of public adjusting.

For practicality across different reproduction methods, including embroidery or screen printing, the logo should also look effective in monochrome, ensuring that it maintains its impact without relying on color gradients.

Typography

In the realm of typography for a public adjusting company, the selection of the right font is pivotal. The chosen font should be a mirror to the brand's character, reflecting the qualities of reliability and professionalism that are essential in this field. Opting for strong, clear fonts can effectively convey these attributes. Readability is another critical factor; the typography must be easily legible across a variety of platforms, ranging from printed materials to digital media. This ensures that the brand's message is effectively communicated in all forms. Additionally, just as with color schemes, the use of typography must be consistent across all branding materials. This consistency is key to maintaining a cohesive and recognizable brand identity, reinforcing the brand's message and values in every visual representation.

If the logo includes text, font choice becomes an important consideration. Fonts should be legible in various sizes and across different reproduction methods, steering clear of overly stylized fonts that may lose clarity in certain formats. The logo's adaptability to different backgrounds is another aspect to consider; it should stand out clearly on both light and dark surfaces, which might require different color variants or a border for enhanced legibility and impact.

Brand Style Guide

Developing a detailed style guide is an essential step for ensuring your brand's visual consistency. This guide should encompass comprehensive guidelines on how to effectively utilize various elements like the logo, color palette, typography, and other key visual components. It's important that this style guide provides clear examples of how these elements should be applied across different types of media. This includes digital platforms, print materials, and physical branding elements, such as office signage or company uniforms, to ensure a unified brand presence. While maintaining consistency is crucial for brand recognition, the style guide should also allow some degree of flexibility and adaptability. This ensures that the brand can stay relevant and effective in different contexts and applications, allowing it to evolve while still retaining its core identity.

Imagery and Graphics

Imagery and graphics are a critical component in the branding of any public adjusting company. You want to choose imagery that speaks directly to the heart of the industry. Think photographs of properties, insurance documents, damaged properties, and other visuals that evoke a strong sense of security and support. These aren't just pictures; they're a narrative tool that tells your clients, "we understand your world."

MARKETING MATERIALS

When we dive into the world of marketing materials, there's a golden rule we need to stick to: consistency. Whether it's your business cards, brochures, or those eye-catching social media posts, every piece should be a reflection of your visual brand guidelines. It's like putting on a well-tailored suit; everything fits just right and looks effortlessly coordinated.

Now, let's talk about the look and feel of these materials. They need to scream professionalism. You're not just selling a service; you're offering peace of mind, expertise, and reliability. That's what a public adjusting firm stands for, and your marketing materials should echo this promise. They are the front line of your brand's image, and they need to make the right impression from the get-go. So, let's make sure they do just that.

Digital Presence

When it comes to your digital presence, consistency is your best friend. Let's bring the same level of visual branding that defines your company to the digital landscape. This means your website, social media profiles, and every post should all sing the same tune. It's all about creating a cohesive and instantly recognizable online presence.

Imagine your clients or potential clients scrolling through their feeds or searching the web; your brand should stand out, making them pause and think, "Ah, that's the trusted public adjusting firm I know!" This uniformity across digital platforms isn't just about looking good — it's about building a strong, reliable brand identity in the digital world where most of our interactions happen these days.

A note on obtaining commercial licenses for fonts, videos, and graphical elements: It's crucial to secure the appropriate legal permissions for all your visual assets, including fonts, videos, and graphical elements, to ensure their lawful use in a commercial setting.

CRAFT YOUR BRAND VOICE

Let's talk about crafting your brand voice, which is essentially the personality of your company in words. For a public adjusting company like yours, the tone of your communication is a big deal. You want to strike the right balance: professional, because you're all about expertise and reliability; empathetic, because you understand what your clients are going through; and authoritative, because, let's face it, you know your stuff and you want your clients to feel they're in capable hands. This voice of yours, it's got to be consistent, whether you're chatting up clients on your website, posting on social media, or sending out emails. It's like being that friend who's always reliable, insightful, and understands just what to say, no matter the platform or situation. That's the kind of voice that resonates with people and builds lasting relationships.

Also, if you are a bi- or trilingual company SAY SO and use it in all forms of your image!!

Create a Brand Story

Let's dive into the art of storytelling, specifically your brand's story. Every company has its saga, a journey of why it started, the hurdles it faced, the victories it celebrated. Yours is no different. It's time to share that story, to unfold the chapters that led to the creation of your public adjusting firm. Why did you start? What challenges did you see in the market that you knew you could tackle? What are those shining moments of success that make you proud? This isn't just about rattling off facts; it's about weaving a narrative that strikes a chord with your audience. A well-told brand story isn't just informative; it's a bridge that connects emotionally with your clients and potential clients. It helps them see beyond a business to the heart and soul of who you are and why you do what you do. That emotional connection? It's pure gold in building lasting relationships and trust.

Implement Branding Across Touch Points

Let's talk about implementing your branding, because it's about more than just a cool logo or a catchy tagline. Your brand identity should be the heartbeat of every customer interaction. Think about it — from the moment someone lands on your website to the way your team handles client service, your brand needs to be front and center. It's like putting on a show where every scene, every character, every line speaks to who you are as a public adjusting firm. Consistency here is key. It's not just about looking uniform; it's about building a level of recognition and trust that only comes when clients know exactly what to expect from you, no matter where or how they interact with your brand. It's this consistency that turns first-time clients into long-time advocates.

ENGAGE THROUGH EVENTS AND WORKSHOPS

Lastly, let's talk about engaging your audience face-to-face. Hosting or participating in events, workshops, or webinars isn't just about imparting knowledge; it's about showing your face, your brand, in action. These gatherings are invaluable for establishing your business as an authority in the field and for engaging directly with potential clients. They're opportunities to shake hands, answer questions, and leave a lasting impression that goes beyond any advertisement.

Remember: marketing in public insurance adjusting isn't a one-size-fits-all endeavor. It's a blend of various channels and tactics, each chosen and tuned to resonate with your specific audience. Your marketing strategy is a living, breathing entity, evolving as your business and your clients do. Keep your ear to the ground, stay adaptable, and watch as your efforts harmonize into success.

BUILD AND MEASURE YOUR MARKETING PLAN

Crafting an effective marketing plan is akin to embarking on a journey of growth and discovery for your business. The starting point? Clearly defined marketing goals. Think of these goals as the signposts that guide you towards your business achievements. They need to be clear and measurable, illuminating the path to your success like a well-lit road in the night.

Establish Key Performance Indicators

Envision KPIs as the milestones along your journey, indicating how far you've come and how close you are to achieving your goals. They're crucial for navigating the landscape of your marketing strategy, ensuring that every action taken is a step closer to your overarching vision. Aligning your marketing efforts with your business objectives ensures that your journey is not just a wander but a purposeful stride towards victory.

KPIs in Action

For public adjusting companies, focusing on marketing efforts that directly impact growth and client acquisition is crucial. Here are several examples of KPIs that can effectively measure the success of marketing initiatives within this niche industry:

◆ **Lead Generation Metrics**

- Number of Qualified Leads: Tracks the total count of potential clients who have shown interest in your services and meet specific criteria that make them likely to become clients.
- Lead Conversion Rate: The percentage of leads that convert into actual clients. This KPI is essential for understanding how effectively your marketing efforts are driving new business.

◆ **Website and Digital Presence**

- Website Traffic: Total number of visitors to your public adjusting company's website. It's a fundamental indicator of your online presence's reach.

- SEO Rankings for Key Terms: Positions of your company's website on search engine results pages (SERPs) for keywords relevant to public adjusting services. Higher rankings can lead to increased visibility and traffic.

◆ **Client Satisfaction and Engagement**

- Net Promoter Score (NPS): A measure of how likely your clients are to recommend your services to others. It's a direct indicator of client satisfaction and loyalty.
- Client Referral Rate: The percentage of clients who refer others to your company over a specific period. High referral rates can indicate satisfied clients and effective client service practices.

◆ **Social Media Engagement**

- Followers and Engagement Rate on Social Platforms: Tracks the number of followers and the level of interaction (likes, shares, comments) with your content on platforms like LinkedIn, Instagram, Twitter/X, and Facebook. These metrics can indicate your brand's reach and how well your content resonates with your audience.

◆ **Content Marketing Effectiveness**

- Content Engagement: Measures how your target audience interacts with your published content, including blog posts, articles, and videos. High engagement rates can indicate relevant and valuable content.

- Downloads of Educational Content: The number of times potential clients download your guides, infographics, one-sheets, or case studies. This KPI can help assess the effectiveness of your content marketing in generating leads.

◆ **Email Marketing Performance**

- Open and Click-Through Rates (CTR): These metrics measure how many recipients open your emails and click on links within them, respectively. They can help evaluate the relevance and appeal of your email content.
- Email List Growth Rate: The rate at which your email subscriber list is growing. This KPI can indicate the effectiveness of lead capture strategies and interest in your company.

◆ **Advertising ROI**

- Return on Advertising Spend (ROAS): This measures the revenue generated for every dollar spent on advertising. It helps public adjusting companies understand the financial effectiveness of their advertising campaigns.

Creating, tracking, and measuring KPIs is a dynamic process that requires alignment with your business objectives, specificity, measurability, relevance, and a clear timeframe. By carefully selecting the right KPIs and employing a structured approach to monitoring them, you can steer your marketing strategy towards achieving tangible results. Remember, the goal is not just to gather data but to glean actionable insights that drive your marketing efforts forward, ensuring your business not only meets but exceeds its goals.

In developing your marketing plan, creativity, strategic thinking, and a deep understanding of your target audience are paramount. It's about charting a unique course that leverages the full spectrum of tools at your disposal to connect with your audience effectively. With a well-thought-out plan, you're not merely competing; you're setting the pace, ready to achieve and surpass your business goals. So, gear up and embark on this journey; the realm of impactful marketing is waiting.

INTEGRATE TRADITIONAL ADVERTISING METHODS

In the digital age, it may be easy to overlook traditional advertising methods. First up is print advertising. It's like rediscovering an old classic novel – timeless and still very much relevant. Utilizing local newspapers, magazines, and industry publications is like placing your message in the hands of your audience, literally. Create visually appealing print ads that tell your brand's story and showcase your unique value proposition. But remember, it's not just about looking good on paper. You've got to keep an eye on the ball, monitoring and measuring the effectiveness of these campaigns. It's like being a detective, searching for clues to understand what resonates with your audience and what doesn't.

Next, we turn the page to networking and community involvement. This is where you step out of the office and into the community. Building relationships with local businesses, insurance agents, and industry professionals is akin to weaving a strong, supportive network. It's about creating connections that are mutually beneficial, where trust and professionalism go hand in hand.

But it's not all handshakes and business cards. Participating in community events and organizations is also about raising your brand awareness. Think of it as becoming a familiar face in the neighborhood, someone people know and respect. And there's more – offering educational seminars or workshops. This is your chance to shine as an industry expert, to share your knowledge and establish your authority. It's about educating your community, about helping them understand what you do and why it matters to them. These seminars aren't just presentations; they're bridges that connect you to your audience, fostering trust and respect.

We've turned the spotlight on traditional advertising methods and community engagement, proving that sometimes, the classic methods are still some of the best tools in our marketing toolbox. Let's not forget the power of a handshake, a community presence, and a well-placed print ad. Remember: in a world rushing towards digitalization, these traditional methods still hold a charm and effectiveness that can be pivotal in building and nurturing lasting relationships with your audience.

RICH'S STORY

MARKETING AND BRANDING STRATEGIES

Rich understood the importance of networking in building his public adjusting business, but he realized he needed additional strategies to reach policyholders directly without constantly trading his time for potential leads. He decided to focus on developing a strong brand and marketing strategy that would effectively communicate his value proposition to potential clients.

Initially, Rich made some missteps in his branding efforts. He tried to appeal to everyone, resulting in a generic message that failed to stand out in the crowded market. His first attempt at a logo was overly complex, and his marketing materials were filled with industry jargon that confused potential clients rather than attracting them.

Recognizing these errors, Rich took a step back and reassessed his approach. He hired a branding consultant who helped him distill his unique selling points and create a clearer, more targeted message. Together, they developed a new brand identity that emphasized Rich's commitment to client advocacy and his expertise in maximizing claim settlements.

Rich also explored various marketing channels. He started a

blog on his website, sharing informative articles about the claims process and tips for policyholders. This not only showcased his expertise but also improved his website's search engine rankings. He created educational videos for social media, explaining common insurance pitfalls and how a public adjuster could help.

To reach a broader audience, Rich invested in targeted online advertising and started a referral program with satisfied clients. He also partnered with local real estate agents and contractors, offering to provide free educational seminars for their clients about property insurance.

These efforts began to pay off. Rich's brand became recognizable in his local market, and potential clients started reaching out to him directly. He found that his marketing strategies were not only attracting more clients but also educating policyholders about the value of public adjusters in general.

While networking remained an important part of his business, Rich's marketing and branding strategies allowed him to reach a wider audience efficiently, setting the stage for sustainable growth.

CHAPTER 8
CLIENT ACQUISITION AND RELATIONSHIPS

Make a customer, not a sale.

KATHERINE BARCHETTI

IN THE COMPETITIVE landscape of public insurance adjusting, the art of acquiring and retaining clients is as crucial as the technical expertise required to manage claims. This chapter delves into the strategies public adjusters, especially those new to client acquisition and marketing principles, can employ to build a strong client base and nurture long-term relationships. The focus is on understanding the target market, developing a comprehensive marketing plan, and implementing effective client retention strategies for sustainable success.

TARGET MARKET

The term "target market" refers to a specific group of consumers or organizations most likely to buy a company's products or services. It's a subset of the broader market a business aims to reach and serve. For public adjusters, the target market would typically consist of policyholders who have experienced property damage and are seeking assistance with their insurance claims.

Defining, identifying, and understanding the public adjuster's target market is not just a marketing tactic; it's a fundamental aspect of their business strategy. It allows them to allocate resources more effectively, offer more personalized and relevant services, and ultimately achieve greater success and sustainability in their practice.

Benefits of Defining the Target Market

Understanding and defining a target market is crucial for several reasons, especially in the context of public adjusters. By determining your target market, you can achieve the following benefits:

- **Efficiency in Marketing Efforts**

By identifying a target market, you can focus your marketing resources on the most relevant and responsive audience. This targeted approach is more cost-effective and efficient than trying to appeal to a broader, less specific group.

- **Tailored Communication and Services**

Knowing the target market allows public adjusters to tailor their communication, services, and overall approach to meet the specific needs, preferences, and pain points of that group. For instance, if a public adjuster identifies homeowners in hurricane-prone areas as a target market, they can customize their services to address common concerns and damages related to hurricanes.

- **Competitive Advantage**

A well-defined target market helps public adjusters differentiate themselves from competitors. By focusing on a particular niche or segment, they can develop specialized expertise and a reputation as the go-to expert for specific types of claims or client groups.

- **Stronger Customer Relationships**

Understanding the target market enables public adjusters to build deeper and more meaningful relationships with their clients. When clients feel that services are tailored to their specific needs, they are more likely to be satisfied, remain loyal, and refer others.

- **Strategic Business Growth**

Identifying and serving a target market effectively can lead to more sustainable business growth. Public adjusters can strategically expand their services or enter new market segments based on informed decisions and a clear understanding of where the demand lies.

- **Enhanced Client Experience**

By focusing on a target market, public adjusters can streamline their processes and client interactions to better suit their clients' preferences, leading to a more positive client experience and higher rates of client retention.

- **Informed Product and Service Development**

Knowledge of the target market guides public adjusters in developing or refining their services. They can identify gaps in the market and introduce services that better meet the evolving needs of their target clients.

REFINING YOUR TARGET MARKET

Once the target market is defined, it is important for the public adjuster to refine the target market more specifically than just "policyholders who have experienced property damage." This is crucial for several reasons. A more refined target market allows for more focused marketing efforts, tailored services, and efficient use of resources. Here are some examples of more refined target markets for public insurance adjusters and the importance of each:

Homeowners in Disaster-Prone Areas

This could include areas frequently affected by natural

disasters like hurricanes, floods, or wildfires. Targeting this market allows adjusters to specialize in claims typical of these events and offer expertise in navigating complex disaster-related claims.

Commercial Property Owners

This group includes owners of buildings used for business purposes, such as retail stores, office buildings, or warehouses. Commercial claims often involve larger sums and more complexities than residential claims, requiring specialized knowledge.

Governmental Entities

This can include public schools, municipal buildings, or other government-owned properties. These entities often have unique insurance needs and face different regulatory requirements, creating a specialized niche for adjusters.

High-Value Residential Properties

Owners of luxury homes or high-value properties often require tailored services due to the high stakes and complexities involved in their insurance claims.

Rental Property Owners

This market includes landlords and real estate investors who own residential or commercial rental properties. They have specific needs related to tenant-occupied properties and loss of rental income claims.

Historic Property Owners

Owners of historic or heritage properties face unique challenges in insurance claims, often needing expertise in dealing with restoration and valuation of historic features.

Policyholders With Specific Types of Claims

This could include specializing in certain types of damage, like water damage, fire damage, hail damage, hurricane damage, flood damage, or mold claims. Specializing in a particular type of claim allows adjusters to develop deep expertise and offer highly specialized services.

FURTHER DEFINING A TARGET MARKET

As your target market becomes more refined and specific, it is important to identify areas where you can further define that target market. Identifying and focusing on more defined target markets is essential for developing expertise, creating effective marketing strategies, improving service delivery, and ultimately, achieving greater success in your business. Areas that you could implemented to further define the target market could include:

Enhanced Expertise and Credibility

Specializing in a particular market allows public adjusters to develop deep expertise in that area, enhancing their credibility and reputation.

Tailored Marketing Strategies

A more defined target market enables adjusters to create more effective, targeted marketing campaigns. Messaging and marketing channels can be tailored to the specific needs and preferences of the target audience.

Improved Service Delivery

Understanding the unique needs of a specific market allows adjusters to tailor their services more effectively, improving client satisfaction and outcomes.

Efficient Resource Allocation

Focusing on a specific target market helps adjusters allocate their time, effort, and resources more efficiently, avoiding the scattergun approach of trying to serve too broad an audience.

Competitive Differentiation

By specializing in a niche market, public adjusters can differentiate themselves from competitors who may offer more generalized services.

Better Client Relationships

A more defined target market allows for building stronger, more personalized relationships with clients, as the services and communication can be more closely aligned with clients' specific needs and circumstances.

WHAT IS THE IDEAL TARGET MARKET FOR A PUBLIC ADJUSTER?

The "best" or "ideal" target market for a public adjuster can vary significantly based on several factors, including the adjuster's expertise, geographic location, and the specific dynamics of the insurance market. However, some general criteria can help define an ideal target market for public adjusters:

High Incidence of Property Claims

Areas or demographics with a high frequency of insurance claims, such as regions prone to natural disasters, are often ideal. In these areas, the demand for public adjuster services is typically higher.

Complex Claims Environments

Target markets where claims are typically complex and involve significant property damage can be ideal. This includes commercial properties, high-value residential properties, or specialized properties like historic buildings. Complex claims often benefit more from the expertise of a public adjuster.

Under-Served or Niche Markets

Markets that are under-served by public adjusters or have specific needs that align with the adjuster's unique skills or experience can be ideal. For example, focusing on a niche like industrial properties or government buildings can be lucrative if there is a demand and limited competition. Areas of concentration with a specific language, such as Haitian Creole or Polish, would greatly benefit from someone who could serve their community and culture.

Policyholders with High-Value or High-Risk Properties

Owners of high-value or high-risk properties are often more invested in ensuring they receive the full benefit of their insurance policies, making them an ideal target market. They are more likely to seek out the services of a public adjuster to maximize their claim recovery.

Educated and Informed Policyholders

Targeting policyholders who understand the value of a public adjuster and are willing to engage their services can lead to more fruitful engagements. These clients are often more cooperative and appreciative of the expertise offered by a public adjuster.

Areas With Favorable Legislation

Regions where laws and regulations are favorable to the work of public adjusters can be an ideal market. In some areas, legal frameworks are more supportive of policyholders hiring public adjusters, which can create a more conducive environment for public adjusters to operate. Some states make public adjusting illegal, and those would never be ideal markets.

Markets with Strong Building Code Standards

States or regions that have established stringent building codes create opportunity for the public adjuster to hold the insurance company to this higher standard. Equally important is that these regions enforce the building code standard.

Demographics with Adequate Insurance Coverage

Targeting demographics that typically have comprehensive insurance coverage and the financial means to pursue claims can lead to more consistent and profitable work. For instance, an area with flood claims but little flood insurance sold, would not be an ideal target market.

Commercial Clients with Ongoing Needs

Businesses or commercial entities that may have ongoing needs for claims assistance, such as property management companies, can provide a steady stream of work and referrals.

HOW TO CONDUCT MARKET RESEARCH AND ANALYSIS

Determining a target market is indeed a multifaceted process that requires a blend of research, analysis, and practical insights. For public adjusters who may not have the resources to conduct this research independently, there are various resources and professionals available to assist. Here's an expanded look at the key methods and resources for identifying a target market:

Demographic Analysis

- Resources

Use online tools, like the US Census Bureau data, real estate databases, and property records to gather demographic information.

- Professionals

Market research firms or freelance data analysts can conduct in-depth demographic analyses, providing detailed reports tailored to your needs.

Industry Claims Trends

- Resources

Industry publications, online forums, and insurance news websites are valuable for staying updated on trends. Subscriptions to services like Insurance Journal or PropertyCasualty360 can be beneficial.

- Professionals

Joining professional associations like NAPIA or AAPIA can provide access to industry reports and expert analyses.

Other Resources

- Resources

Survey tools like SurveyMonkey or Google Forms can be used to gather psychographic data. Social media insights and analytics tools can also provide valuable information about the attitudes and preferences of potential clients.

- Professionals

Marketing consultants or consumer behavior specialists can

offer deeper insights into the psychographic profiles of potential clients.

UNDERSTANDING COMPETITORS' STRATEGIES

Analyzing competitors' marketing strategies, client communication, and engagement methods can provide insights into what works well in the market and what doesn't.

Cost-Effective Market Insights

Competitive analysis is a relatively inexpensive way to gain market insights. Much of the information about competitors can be gathered through online research, client feedback, and observation of market trends.

This method of research is less costly compared to primary market research methods, like surveys or focus groups.

Adapting To Changing Market Conditions

Regular competitive analysis helps public adjusters stay agile and adapt to changing market conditions. By keeping an eye on how competitors evolve, adjusters can anticipate market shifts and adjust their strategies accordingly.

Identification of Market Gaps

Review of competitor's approach to the market can reveal areas of opportunity for the public adjuster.

Benchmarking and Differentiation

Competitive analysis allows public adjusters to benchmark their services against those of their competitors. This helps in understanding how they stack up in terms of service quality, client satisfaction, and expertise.

It also aids in identifying unique selling propositions (USPs) that can differentiate a public adjuster's services from others in the market, which is crucial for branding and marketing.

Informed Decision-Making

The insights gained from a competitive analysis can inform various aspects of a public adjuster's business strategy, from marketing and client acquisition to service development and pricing. It helps in making data-driven decisions that are aligned with market realities.

CREATE MARKETING STRATEGIES TO ATTRACT AND RETAIN CLIENTS

Marketing is not just a tool; it's the lifeblood of your business. It's how you capture the attention of potential clients, elevate your brand, and clearly communicate the unique value you bring to the table. Remember, successful marketing is more than just visibility – it's about strategic connections and lasting impressions.

Understand Your Audience

The first rule of effective marketing? Know your audience inside out. This means revisiting and constantly updating your market research. Understanding your target clients' needs, preferences, and pain points isn't just helpful; it's essential. Every piece of your marketing puzzle should be tailored to resonate with them. After all, a message that hits home is far more powerful than a broad, scattergun approach.

Communicate Your Value

Your value proposition is your battle cry. It needs to be loud and clear in all your marketing efforts. What unique benefits does your public adjusting business offer? How do you stand out in handling policyholder claims? These are the questions your marketing materials need to answer unequivocally. It's about making sure your potential clients know exactly why they should choose you.

Embrace a Multi-Channel Approach

Gone are the days of one-track marketing. To really make your mark, you need a multi-channel approach. This means weaving together digital strategies like social media, email campaigns, and search engine optimization (SEO) with traditional tactics such as direct mail or local ads. It's about meeting your clients where they are, in the digital world and beyond.

The Power of Content Marketing

Content is king, and in the world of public adjusting, it's your most persuasive ambassador. High-quality, informative content that addresses common insurance queries and concerns can position you as an industry thought leader. Whether it's through insightful blog posts, informative articles, engaging videos, or interactive webinars, your content marketing should educate and captivate your audience.

Solidify Your Online Presence

In today's digital era, a strong online presence is non-negotiable. Your website should be a beacon, drawing clients with its user-friendly design and wealth of information. Showcase your services, client testimonials, and valuable educational resources. And don't forget about SEO – optimizing your site for search engines is crucial for ensuring that when potential clients are looking, they find you first. Even if you obtain the majority of your clients via word-of-mouth, those potential customers are going to your website and social media properties to vet you and your results. Don't let them find nothing, or worse yet, a GoDaddy landing page.

In summary, effective marketing in public adjusting isn't just about being seen; it's about creating a connection, delivering value, and establishing trust. Remember: your marketing strategy is your road map to not just attracting clients — it is foundational to attracting clients, converting to them to customers, and forging relationships that last.

DEVELOP A SALES PLAN TO GENERATE LEADS AND CONVERT THEM INTO CUSTOMERS

Some of the best clients you will ever get is by referrals. But when you are starting out, you need to start someplace.

Developing a sales plan is more than just plotting points on a graph or knocking on doors. It's about understanding your market, crafting a process that works, and empowering those who represent your brand. Bear in mind that your sales strategy is a dynamic, evolving entity, one that requires attention, adaptation, and a keen understanding of the ever-changing dance of client needs and market trends.

Invest in Sales Training

If your arsenal includes a sales team, or even adjusters that bring in their own claims, remember that their skills and knowledge are as vital as how many doors they knock on. Investing in their training is not just about honing their selling abilities. It's about equipping them to be ambassadors of your brand, adept at communicating your value proposition and turning leads into loyal clients. This investment isn't just a cost; it's planting seeds that will grow into the fruitful trees of future business.

Strategies for Lead Generation

Let's start with the lifeblood of any sales plan – lead generation. Identifying strategies that resonate with your target audience is like finding the right key for a lock. This could mean rubbing elbows at industry events, building a network that turns every handshake into a potential opportunity, launching captivating online ad campaigns, or forming strategic alliances with related businesses. It's about putting your brand in the spotlight, making sure that when a potential client needs someone with your expertise, you're the first name that comes to mind.

Streamline the Sales Process

Now, let's talk about the sales process. This is your playbook, detailing every move from the first contact with a lead to the final handshake of a deal. It's crucial to have this process clearly defined. If you have a sales team, this becomes their script. Training them in this process ensures everyone sings from the same hymn sheet, guaranteeing consistency and effectiveness in every interaction.

Master the Art of Lead Conversion

Having a meticulously crafted sales plan isn't just advantageous – it's essential. Consider this chapter your guide to creating a blueprint for your sales efforts, a road map that not only guides you to your destination but ensures you enjoy the journey.

UTILIZING VARIOUS MARKETING CHANNELS AND TACTICS TO REACH THE TARGET AUDIENCE

Think of effective marketing as a rock band — each channel and tactic plays its part to create a jam that resonates with your audience. This chapter is about mastering that mix in addition to boots-on-the-ground relationship building, ensuring that each note hits just right.

Online Marketing and Social Media

First, let's dive into the digital ocean — online marketing. Platforms like Facebook, LinkedIn, Nextdoor, and others aren't just social spaces; they're vibrant communities where potential clients live and engage. Your mission? To be a part of these communities, offering compelling content that doesn't just sell but educates and builds trust. It's about starting conversations, sharing insights, and establishing your brand as a trusted advisor in the maze of insurance claims.

The Power of Email Marketing

Now, onto a classic but potent tool – email marketing. Building an email list is like gathering a crowd of interested listeners. Regular emails to this list are your chance to talk directly to them, offering valuable nuggets of wisdom, tips, and updates on insurance claims handling. This isn't just about filling their inbox; it's about enriching their knowledge and keeping your brand top of mind.

ENHANCING CLIENT ACQUISITION AND RETENTION

Understanding the competitive landscape helps in crafting more effective client acquisition strategies. By knowing what competitors offer, public adjusters can tailor their messaging to highlight how their services are superior or more suited to potential clients' needs.

It also aids in client retention, as adjusters can continuously refine their offerings to ensure they are providing top-tier services compared to competitors.

Completing a competitive analysis is an extremely important step for public adjusters, as it provides a wealth of information about the market, competitors, and potential opportunities in an efficient and cost-effective manner. It enables public adjusters to identify gaps in the market, understand how to differentiate themselves, and make informed decisions that contribute to the success and growth of their business.

DIGITAL RESOURCES FOR INDUSTRY INSIGHTS

Subscriptions to Industry Publications

Digital subscriptions to industry publications, like *Insurance Journal* or *PropertyCasualty360*, offer a wealth of information, including market analyses, regulatory changes, and emerging trends in the property insurance claim sector.

Online Forums, Blogs, and Social Media

Platforms, like LinkedIn groups, Facebook industry groups, insurance forums, and other social media channels, can provide real-time insights into industry trends, peer discussions, expert opinions, and opposition views. Listserv discussions among insurance company adjusters indicate geographic areas of need, suggesting property-loss opportunities for public adjusters. Let's not forget Chip's own *Property Insurance Coverage Law Blog* for timely industry updates.

LEVERAGE PROFESSIONAL ASSOCIATIONS FOR MARKET INTELLIGENCE

Membership in Professional Associations

Associations like NAPIA or AAPIA (or any state or regional association) often have access to exclusive market research, industry reports, expert analyses, forms, and letter templates. They may also host webinars and conferences featuring industry leaders discussing current trends and future predictions.

Networking for Insights

Engaging with peers, experts, and consultants through these associations can provide anecdotal evidence and practical insights that complement formal research.

Referral Program

Develop a program that encourages satisfied clients to refer others to your services. This could include incentives or recognition for clients who refer new business to you. Referrals are a powerful tool as they come with the trust and credibility of the referrer already established. *Please make certain that the referral program complies with state regulations and limitations.* A strong referral program can be a cost-effective way to obtain new clients.

RICH'S STORY

CLIENT ACQUISITION AND RELATIONSHIP

Rich's journey in client acquisition and relationship building was marked by a profound shift in perspective. He realized that success in public adjusting wasn't just about signing contracts and collecting checks, but about forging meaningful connections with clients he genuinely enjoyed working with. This epiphany transformed his approach to business development.

Rich began to view each potential client not as a transaction, but as a unique individual facing a challenging time in their life. He invested time in understanding the personal impact of property losses on his clients, recognizing that empathy was as crucial as expertise in his role. This approach not only helped him provide better service but also fostered deeper, more rewarding professional relationships.

He developed a knack for active listening, allowing clients to share their concerns and experiences fully. This not only helped Rich tailor his services more effectively but also built trust and rapport. He found that clients appreciated his genuine interest in their well-being beyond just the claim process.

Rich's commitment to understanding the broader impact of losses on his clients' lives or businesses led to more comprehensive and satisfying resolutions. His clients felt truly supported, not just in navigating their claims, but in rebuilding their lives or operations.

This client-centric approach naturally led to an increase in referrals. Satisfied clients, touched by Rich's genuine care and effective service, eagerly recommended him to others in similar situations. Rich found that these referrals often resulted in relationships with clients who shared his values and appreciation for a personalized approach.

As his business grew, Rich maintained this focus on quality relationships over quantity of contracts. He discovered that working with clients he connected with not only made his work more fulfilling but also contributed significantly to his professional success and personal satisfaction.

CHAPTER 9
BUILD YOUR CLAIM HANDLING AND OFFICE SUPPORT TEAM

> Talent wins games, but teamwork and intelligence win championships.
>
> MICHAEL JORDAN

IN A PUBLIC ADJUSTING, establishing a successful business lies in crafting a team that is not only competent and efficient but also deeply committed to delivering exceptional service to clients. This chapter delves into the critical process of identifying, assembling, and nurturing a team equipped to handle the multifaceted challenges of the public adjusting landscape.

UNDERSTAND ROLES AND RESPONSIBILITIES

The journey begins with a deep dive into the various tasks and functions integral to claim handling and office support. It's imperative to recognize that the role of a claim handling professional extends beyond mere damage assessment and negotiations with insurance companies. It encompasses a comprehensive suite of responsibilities including meticulous documentation, robust client communication, and diligent follow-ups. Similarly, office support staff are the backbone of the business, ensuring seamless operations through tasks like scheduling, record maintenance, and correspondence management.

Deepen Role Specialization and Collaboration

Understanding the intricacies of each role within your public adjusting firm allows for a more nuanced approach to team building. For instance, claim adjusters might specialize further based on types of claims — such as residential, commercial, or catastrophic loss—allowing for deeper expertise in each domain. Similarly, fostering a culture of collaboration across different roles enhances the team's ability to provide holistic solutions to clients. Encouraging regular cross-functional meetings and joint problem-solving sessions can bridge gaps in understanding and improve overall service delivery.

Craft a Cohesive Team Structure

A well-rounded public adjusting firm requires a blend of roles including claim adjusters, administrative support, customer service representatives, and depending on claim complexity, legal advisors or construction experts. The key to a smooth workflow lies in understanding how each role contributes to the overall mission of the company and ensuring these roles are filled by individuals who are not only skilled but also passionate about their contribution to the client's journey.

Assigning specific responsibilities and required skills for each role is crucial. A claim adjuster, for example, should have a comprehensive grasp of insurance policies, adeptness in damage assessment, and formidable negotiation skills. Administrative staff need to excel in organization, be proficient with office software, and possess exemplary communication skills. The synergy within the team, fueled by individual competencies and collaborative spirit, forms the bedrock of operational excellence.

Leverage Technology for Efficiency and Client Engagement

Implementing state-of-the-art technology solutions like ClaimWizard can significantly boost your team's efficiency and effectiveness. ClaimWizard, for example, can streamline the entire claims process, from documentation to settlement, freeing up your team to focus on more complex aspects of claim resolution. Additionally, adopting client engagement platforms can enhance communication with clients, providing them with real-time updates and fostering transparency throughout the claim handling process.

ASSESS AND ADAPT TEAM COMPOSITION

Understanding the volume and complexity of claims your business handles is essential for determining the ideal team size and composition. This involves evaluating the current workload distribution to identify potential overburdened areas or inefficiencies, thereby adjusting team size or reallocating tasks to ensure optimal performance.

Training and Development

Developing role-specific training programs is a critical next step, ensuring that every team member is equipped with the latest knowledge and tools to excel in their respective roles. For claim adjusters, this might include updates on policy changes or new damage assessment technologies. For support staff, training could focus on mastering claim management software or honing customer service skills.

Advanced Training and Continuous Professional Development

Elevating the skill set of your team involves committing to advanced training programs and continuous professional development opportunities (for more on professional development, see Chapter 13 — Professional Development). This could include certifications in public adjusting, advanced negotiation workshops, or training in cutting-edge technologies such as drone assessments or 3D imaging for damage inspections. Encouraging team members to attend industry conferences or participate in webinars not only keeps them abreast of the latest trends but also stimulates innovative thinking and best practice sharing.

Foster a Culture of Excellence and Adaptability

Promoting a culture of continuous learning and process efficiency can significantly enhance team productivity and service quality. Encouraging versatility among team members ensures that the team can adapt to varying demands with agility and competence.

Scale Your Team for Future Growth

Anticipating the needs of a growing business and planning for scalability in your team structure is crucial. This might mean maintaining a core team while supplementing with part-time or contract workers during peak periods, ensuring the flexibility to adjust to fluctuating workloads.

Strategic Workload Management and Team Scaling

An analytical approach to workload management involves not just assessing current capacities but also forecasting future needs based on market trends and potential growth areas. This strategic perspective might lead to the development of specialized teams dedicated to emerging risk areas or the adoption of methodologies to enhance responsiveness and adaptability. Scaling the team, therefore, becomes a strategic decision aligned with long-term business goals, ensuring that your firm is not just reacting to the market but actively shaping its approach to meet future demands.

Build a Team Aligned with Your Values

Hiring individuals who not only possess the necessary skills but also embody the values and ethos of your business is vital.

Promoting a collaborative work environment and open communication fosters a united team, dedicated to advocating for clients and delivering superior service.

Cultivate a Strong Team Culture and Ethos

Creating an environment where every team member feels valued and understood goes a long way in building a resilient and dedicated team. This involves recognizing individual achievements, supporting work-life balance, and fostering an inclusive culture where diversity of thought and background is celebrated. Encouraging mentorship programs within your firm can also help in transferring knowledge, enhancing skill sets, and strengthening the bonds between team members.

By embracing these expanded strategies for team building and development, your public adjusting firm not only solidifies its position in the present but also paves the way for sustained success and growth in the future. Your team, with its blend of expertise, innovation, and client-centric focus, becomes the most valuable asset in navigating the complexities of the insurance claims landscape, driving forward with confidence and vision.

RECRUITING AND HIRING

Developing a strategic hiring plan is more than just an operational necessity for a public adjusting firm; it's a pivotal step towards shaping the future and ethos of your organization. It's not merely about filling vacancies but about inviting new members into your professional family who will champion your firm's mission and contribute to its legacy. Let's explore how to craft this plan with a blend of precision, foresight, and a dash of creativity.

Set the Stage: Define Hiring Objectives

Begin with clarity and intention. Ask yourself, "What are the specific needs of my firm?" Whether it's bringing in seasoned professionals with a wealth of experience in complex claims or versatile talents adept at wearing multiple hats, having a crystal-clear objective will act as your North Star. This clarity ensures your recruitment efforts are laser-focused on attracting individuals who align with your firm's strategic goals and cultural ethos.

Craft Your Blueprint: Comprehensive Hiring Strategy

Consider your hiring strategy as the blueprint for building your dream team. This blueprint should reflect your firm's core values and the cultural fabric that holds your team together. It's about finding those gems who are not only technically proficient but who also resonate with your firm's commitment to fairness, integrity, and unwavering client advocacy. The channels you choose, from niche job boards to professional networking events, should be conduits for connecting with these like-minded professionals.

Hire people with integrity. Warren Buffet provided this advice when hiring:

> We look for three things when we hire people. We look for intelligence, we look for initiative or energy, and we look for integrity. And if they don't have the latter, the first two will kill you, because if you're going to get someone without integrity, you want them lazy and dumb.

Lay the Foundations: Job Descriptions and Recruitment Methods

Creating job descriptions is akin to laying the foundations of your hiring plan. Each description should serve as a beacon, attracting candidates by clearly delineating roles, expectations, and the skills required. But it's not just about the nuts and bolts of the job; it's your opportunity to communicate your firm's mission and the values you hold dear, turning a job listing into a call to arms for those who share your dedication to justice and client service.

Diversifying your recruitment methods enriches your candidate pool, bringing a wealth of perspectives and expertise to your doorstep. Embrace a multi-channel approach, tapping into everything from online platforms to word-of-mouth referrals within your professional network. Remember, the best candidates are often those who aren't actively looking but can be swayed by the right opportunity.

Perfect the Art of Selection: Interviews and Cultural Fit

Interviewing is where the magic happens—it's your chance to peer beneath the resume and glimpse the person behind the professional. Craft an interview process that tests not just technical prowess but also the soft skills that are so crucial in this industry, such as empathy, communication, and adaptability. Incorporate real-world scenarios or case studies to see how candidates think on their feet.

However, skills and experience are only part of the puzzle. A candidate's ability to mesh with your team's culture and values is equally important. Look for signs of a shared ethos and a genuine passion for client advocacy, as these are the traits that will enrich your team and enhance your firm's reputation.

Build for Tomorrow: Flexibility and Growth Opportunities

In the fast-evolving world of public adjusting, your hiring plan needs the flexibility to pivot as new trends emerge and client needs evolve. Regularly revisiting and adjusting your hiring strategy ensures your team remains at the forefront of the industry.

Highlighting opportunities for professional growth within your firm can be a major draw for top talent. Ambitious professionals are always looking for ways to advance their skills and careers. Showcasing your commitment to continuous learning and development can set your firm apart as a place where careers flourish.

Cement Your Reputation: Employer Brand and Team Involvement

Your firm's reputation as an employer is invaluable. A strong employer brand that reflects your dedication to excellence, employee welfare, and ethical practices will naturally attract individuals who share those values. Let your current team members be ambassadors of your brand, sharing their experiences and insights with potential candidates.

Involving your team in the recruitment process not only provides diverse perspectives but also helps assess how well candidates will integrate with your existing dynamics. This collective approach ensures new hires are not just a good fit on paper but will truly enhance your team's cohesion and spirit.

The Final Touch: Prioritize Candidate Experience

The recruitment process is also a reflection of your firm's professionalism and values. Ensuring a positive experience for every candidate, from clear communication to respectful interactions, speaks volumes about your firm's integrity and respect for individuals. This positive engagement can enhance your firm's standing in the industry, making it a sought-after place to work.

In conclusion, crafting a strategic hiring plan is a journey that goes beyond mere recruitment; it's about curating a team that embodies the ideals and values your public adjusting firm stands for. By approaching this process with a clear vision, a commitment to diversity, and a focus on cultural fit, you'll build not just a team, but a community of professionals dedicated to making a difference in the lives of those you serve. This, in turn, is not just good for business; it's good for the soul of your organization.

Mike Michalowicz's book *All In* offers essential insights into improving hiring processes for business owners. It details how to identify candidates who match company culture, develop effective interviewing techniques, and implement efficient hiring and onboarding strategies. This comprehensive guide helps entrepreneurs create a skilled and cohesive team that contributes to business success.

ONBOARDING AND TRAINING

Creating an effective onboarding process is like setting the stage for a grand performance, where each new hire plays a crucial role in the success of your public insurance adjusting firm. It's a dynamic mix of welcoming new talents into the fold and equipping them with the tools, knowledge, and understanding they need to excel from the get-go. Let's unpack how to make this process as impactful and nurturing as possible.

Craft an Onboarding Plan

Think of your onboarding plan as the blueprint for success. It's not just a checklist; it's a comprehensive road map that guides new hires through the initial weeks or months. Start with a warm welcome that makes them feel part of the team immediately. Then, introduce them to key team members and walk them through a meticulously planned schedule of training activities. The objective? To transition them from newcomers to integral parts of the team smoothly and effectively.

Embed Them in Your Culture

Your firm's culture is the heartbeat of your operation. It's what sets you apart and binds your team together. Use the onboarding process as an opportunity to immerse new hires in your firm's values, ethos, and the way these principles manifest in day-to-day operations. Discuss your unwavering commitment to client advocacy, the highest ethical standards, and the power of teamwork. Setting these expectations early on lays the foundation for their future actions and decisions.

Claim Handling and Support Processes

A deep dive into your firm's claim handling processes and support systems is essential. Provide a bird's-eye view of how things work, from initial client contact to claim resolution, and show them where they fit within this ecosystem. This comprehensive understanding is crucial for them to start making meaningful contributions swiftly.

Comprehensive Training

Equipping your team with the right tools is non-negotiable. Whether it's mastering claim management software or navigating the intricacies of claim assessment, offer hands-on training to ensure they're up to speed with the technology and methodologies they'll be using daily. But it doesn't stop there. Best practices in claim handling, from evaluating claims to client communication and negotiation tactics, are equally vital. Tap into the wealth of knowledge within your team to mentor and guide them through these early stages.

Cultivate a Culture of Continuous Improvement

The landscape of insurance is ever-evolving, demanding constant adaptation and learning. Encourage active participation in the broader industry through conferences and workshops. Facilitate access to a wealth of educational resources and underscore the value of ongoing professional development. It's about fostering a mindset where growth and learning are continuous.

Team Building and Mentorship

Incorporate team-building activities to weave new hires into the fabric of your team, promoting a sense of unity and shared purpose. Pairing them with experienced mentors can also turbocharge their learning and integration, providing a personal touch to their developmental journey.

Feedback and Customization

Regular check-ins are your radar system, helping you gauge how well new hires are adjusting and where they might need more support or resources. Tailor the training to fit their unique backgrounds and learning paces, recognizing that one size does not fit all. Simulations and real-world scenarios can make training more relatable and engaging, while leveraging technology can offer flexibility and a varied learning experience.

Build a Knowledge-Sharing Ecosystem

Promote an environment where knowledge sharing is not just encouraged but celebrated. This could take many forms, from formal presentations to casual lunch-and-learn sessions. It's about creating a community of learners and experts who support each other's growth and success.

Their Continuous Journey

Remember, onboarding is just the beginning of a journey. It's about setting the stage for ongoing development, engagement, and success. By investing in a robust onboarding and continuous learning program, you're not just nurturing your team's skills; you're reinforcing a culture of excellence, collaboration, and client-focused service. In the realm of public insurance adjusting, where the depth of your team's expertise and their commitment to advocacy can significantly impact your clients' lives, a well-conceived onboarding process is not just beneficial; it's essential. It's your firm's first step towards building a legacy of excellence and a team that stands as a testament to your commitment to serving those in need with integrity, expertise, and compassion.

COLLABORATION AND COMMUNICATION

In a public adjusting company, where the intricacies of claim handling intertwine with the art of client communication, establishing a culture of clear and effective communication is not just beneficial—it's essential. It's about weaving a tapestry of success, with each thread representing a team member, a process, or a value that your firm holds dear. Let's dive deeper into creating this culture, ensuring that every new hire and seasoned professional alike contributes to a harmonious and productive workplace.

Lay the Foundation: Implementing Effective Communication Channels

The backbone of effective team interaction lies in selecting and utilizing the right communication channels. Imagine your team as a well-tuned orchestra, where each instrument's sound is distinct yet harmoniously blended. From the precision of emails to the immediacy of internal messaging platforms and the warmth of face-to-face conversations, each channel serves a purpose. It's about striking the right balance, ensuring that messages are not just sent but also received, understood, and acted upon with clarity and efficiency.

Cultivate a Garden of Ideas: Encourage Open Dialogue

Fostering an environment where feedback flows freely and suggestions are welcomed with open arms is like nurturing a garden of ideas—diverse, vibrant, and full of potential. This openness not only sparks innovation but also fortifies the team, making every member feel valued and heard. It's about creating a space where constructive dialogue flourishes, paving the way for continuous improvement and a strong, unified team spirit.

The Digital Toolbox: Utilizing Project Management Tools and Software

In the realm of public adjusting, where complexity meets urgency, leveraging technology to streamline communication is key. Tools like ClaimWizard become the digital toolbox that keeps everyone aligned, organized, and informed. These platforms are the virtual meeting rooms, the filing cabinets, and the project trackers rolled into one, ensuring that no detail is overlooked, and every deadline is met with precision.

Build Bridges: Foster Collaboration and Teamwork

Encouraging collaboration among team members is akin to building bridges—connecting diverse skills, experiences, and perspectives to achieve common goals. It's about championing a culture where teamwork is the norm, and every member supports and uplifts the others. This collaborative spirit is especially crucial in navigating the complexities of large or intricate claims, where the collective expertise can lead to innovative solutions and superior outcomes.

A Mosaic of Talents: Promoting a Supportive and Inclusive Team Culture

Creating an inclusive team culture is like crafting a mosaic—each piece unique yet part of a beautiful whole. This means valuing each member's contribution, embracing diverse viewpoints, and nurturing a supportive environment where professional growth is encouraged. Such a culture not only enhances team morale but also drives better results for clients, reflecting the very best of what your firm stands for.

The Pulse of the Team: Regular Meetings and Check-Ins

Just as a regular pulse is a sign of a healthy heart, regular team meetings and check-ins are indicators of a healthy team dynamic. These gatherings serve as a forum for sharing updates, discussing challenges, and aligning on goals. They ensure that every team member, from the newest recruit to the most seasoned veteran, is moving in the same direction, fueled by a shared purpose and commitment.

Navigate Challenges: Resolve Conflicts and Foster a Positive Work Environment

Even in the most harmonious teams, conflicts can arise. Establishing a clear conflict resolution process is like having a navigational chart that guides you through turbulent waters, ensuring that disagreements are addressed constructively and resolved swiftly. Coupled with a positive and respectful work environment, this approach not only minimizes disruptions but also strengthens the team's resilience and cohesiveness.

Personal Touch: Tailor Communication to Individual Preferences

Understanding and respecting individual communication preferences is like fine-tuning an instrument to produce the perfect sound. Recognizing that some team members may prefer in-depth discussions while others thrive on quick, concise updates allows for more effective and comfortable interactions. This personalized approach not only enhances efficiency but also shows respect for each team member's working style.

The Continuum of Learning: Integrating Communication Training

Investing in communication training is investing in the lifeline of your team's success. Effective communication—be it through active listening, empathetic engagement, or clear articulation—is a skill that benefits every aspect of your team's operations. Workshops and training sessions focused on these skills can significantly bolster your team's ability to work cohesively, navigate challenges, and deliver exceptional service to your clients.

In crafting a culture of effective communication and collaboration within your public adjusting firm, you're doing more than just enhancing internal processes; you're laying the groundwork for sustained success, client satisfaction, and a positive workplace environment. Remember, at the heart of every successful claim resolution and satisfied client is a team that communicates clearly, collaborates effectively, and supports one another unwaveringly. By prioritizing these principles, you ensure that your firm not only stands out in the competitive landscape of public adjusting but also becomes a place where professionals grow, thrive, and contribute to their fullest potential.

MANAGE PERFORMANCE AND PRODUCTIVITY

In the world of public insurance adjusting, the strength and efficiency of your team are paramount. It's like navigating a ship through ever-changing seas—the clearer the direction and the better the crew's understanding of their roles and responsibilities, the smoother the journey. Let's dive deeper into setting performance goals and expectations that not only propel your firm forward but also ensure a rewarding journey for every team member.

Establish Clear Performance Goals

Imagine setting sail without a map; that's what working without clear goals can feel like. Start by charting a clear course for each team member, ensuring these goals are as specific and measurable as the stars used for navigation. For instance, a claim adjuster might aim to increase customer satisfaction scores by a certain percentage or reduce the average claim processing time. This specificity helps team members focus their efforts and truly understand their impact on the firm's voyage.

Define Key Performance Indicators (KPIs)

KPIs are the guiding stars that keep your team on course. They illuminate the path to success, providing quantifiable metrics that align with both the individual's role and the overarching goals of your firm. Whether it's the speed of claim resolution or the accuracy of assessments, these KPIs offer a clear view of where the journey is on track and where adjustments might be needed.

Align Individual Goals with Business Objectives

The synergy between individual ambitions and the firm's mission is crucial. Like a crew working in unison, when each member understands how their efforts contribute to the larger goals, the sense of purpose and motivation runs deep. This alignment not only enhances individual performance but also propels the firm towards its overarching objectives.

Regular Feedback and Performance Evaluations

Journeys are filled with learning opportunities, and regular performance evaluations serve as navigational checkpoints. These moments allow for reflection, adjustment, and recognition. Constructive feedback, provided with an eye towards growth and encouragement, ensures that every team member knows how to steer their efforts for better alignment with their goals and the firm's trajectory.

Recognize and Reward Outstanding Performance

Recognition acts as the wind in the sails, motivating the team to push forward. Celebrating milestones and outstanding performances not only boosts morale but also reinforces the behaviors and efforts that lead to success. Whether it's through bonuses, public acknowledgment, or professional growth opportunities, recognizing achievements is key to fostering a motivated and dedicated crew.

Address Performance Issues

When the waters get rough, a proactive approach is necessary. Addressing performance issues early and with a supportive mindset ensures minor setbacks don't turn into major obstacles. Offering resources for improvement, whether through additional training or mentorship, shows your commitment to each team member's success and development.

Regular use of performance metrics and feedback mechanisms can help identify areas where a public adjuster may be struggling. This might include periodic reviews of case handling, client feedback, and peer evaluations. Early detection allows for timely interventions, preventing small issues from evolving into larger problems that could impact client satisfaction and settlements.

Feedback should be framed positively, focusing on how the adjuster can grow rather than solely on what went wrong. For instance, instead of saying "You failed to communicate effectively with the client," try "Enhancing your communication skills could further increase client trust and satisfaction."

NAVIGATE TEAM GROWTH

The world of public insurance adjusting is ever-evolving, and so too should be the skills and knowledge of your team.

Encouraging continuous learning and professional development ensures your crew is always ready to meet the challenges ahead. From workshops to certifications, investing in your team's growth is investing in the firm's future.

Customize Goals and Support

Recognize that each team member's journey is unique. Tailoring goals to leverage individual strengths and address areas for growth ensures that everyone can navigate their path successfully. Providing support that matches each person's needs and learning style fosters a team that's not only skilled but also resilient and adaptable.

Incorporate Flexibility into Goal Setting

The sea of public adjusting is full of unexpected turns. Incorporating flexibility into your goal-setting process allows your team to adapt to industry changes and unforeseen challenges. This agility ensures that goals remain relevant and achievable, no matter how the tides may turn.

OFFICE SUPPORT TOOLS AND SYSTEMS

Efficiency translates directly into client satisfaction and operational success. Embracing technology is not just beneficial — it's imperative. Implementing efficient claim management systems forms the backbone of a high-performing insurance adjusting firm, setting the stage for streamlined operations and enhanced service delivery. Let's navigate through the process of integrating these systems into your firm, ensuring that every step leads to greater efficiency and better outcomes for your clients.

Choose the Right Software: The Cornerstone of Efficiency

The quest for the perfect claim management software is akin to finding the right compass for a voyage. It should guide your firm through the complexities of claim handling with ease and precision. When evaluating software options, prioritize solutions designed with the unique needs of public adjusting in mind, such as ClaimWizard. Key considerations should include ease of use, the ability to integrate with existing tools, and scalability to grow with your business. This ensures that the software not only meets your current needs but also adapts to future challenges.

Harness Automation: The Path to Enhanced Productivity

In the realm of claim management, automation is your steadfast ally, capable of transforming time-consuming tasks into swift, error-free processes. From automating data entry and claim tracking to generating reports at the click of a button, automation frees your team from the mundane, allowing them to dedicate their expertise to more complex, client-focused tasks. It's about optimizing efficiency without sacrificing the personal touch that defines your service.

Safeguard Data: The Keystone of Trust

In an industry built on trust, ensuring the security and confidentiality of client data is paramount. Opt for systems that not only comply with the highest standards of data security but also actively protect against emerging threats. Regular security audits and updates should be non-negotiable, safeguarding your firm's reputation and your clients' trust.

Streamline Operations with Productivity Tools

Leveraging the right set of productivity tools can significantly streamline your firm's operations. From claim management software to communication and document management platforms, these tools work in concert to create a seamless workflow. They not only enhance efficiency but also ensure that every team member has the resources they need to excel in their role.

Foster Team Collaboration

The digital age offers unparalleled opportunities for collaboration, breaking down barriers and bringing teams closer together, regardless of physical location. Utilize digital tools to foster a collaborative environment where information is shared freely, and teamwork is not just encouraged but ingrained in your firm's culture.

Training: Empower Your Team

The implementation of new systems is only as effective as the team behind them. Invest in thorough training programs to ensure that every team member is adept at using the technology at their disposal. This investment pays dividends in the form of increased productivity, fewer errors, and a team that feels confident and supported.

Offer tailored training sessions that focus on areas needing improvement, such as negotiation skills, legal aspects of claims, or customer service and communications. Workshops can be led by experienced adjusters, external experts, lawyers or even vendors with particular knowledge of claim issues.

Training time and cost should be thought of as an investment rather than an expense.

Implement 360-Degree Feedback

A 360-degree feedback system is like gathering insights from all directions—peers, supervisors, and subordinates alike. This comprehensive perspective provides valuable feedback that can highlight areas of strength and opportunities for improvement, ensuring every team member has a full view of their performance and impact.

By setting clear, achievable goals and providing regular, constructive feedback, you create a culture of continuous improvement and success. Recognizing and rewarding performance, addressing challenges proactively, and supporting professional growth are all crucial steps in ensuring your team not only meets but exceeds their performance goals. In the competitive and complex field of public insurance adjusting, a well-guided, motivated, and skilled team is your greatest asset. Remember, the journey towards excellence is ongoing, and with each step, your firm not only moves closer to its goals but also builds a legacy of dedication, integrity, and outstanding service to your clients.

Celebrating Together: Recognizing Achievements and Teamwork

Acknowledging and celebrating team achievements is like gathering for a feast after a successful harvest—it's a time to reflect on the hard work, dedication, and teamwork that led to those successes. Whether it's a major milestone or a small victory, recognizing these achievements reinforces the value of collaboration and hard work, boosting morale and fostering a sense of pride and unity among team members.

Keeping Your Systems Shipshape: The Importance of Regular Reviews

Just as a ship requires regular maintenance to navigate the seas smoothly, your claim management systems necessitate ongoing reviews to ensure they remain aligned with your firm's evolving needs. Stay abreast of technological advancements and be ready to adapt, ensuring your systems continue to offer the best possible support to your team and clients.

Tailoring Solutions: The Custom Fit

While off-the-shelf solutions can meet many of your needs, customizing these tools to better fit the specific demands of your business can significantly enhance their effectiveness. Work closely with software providers to tailor features that address your firm's unique challenges, ensuring your technology solutions are as bespoke as the service you provide to your clients.

Embracing the Cloud: For Flexibility and Accessibility

Cloud-based solutions such as ClaimWizard offer a world of flexibility, allowing your team to access vital information and collaborate in real-time, no matter where they are. This is especially crucial for adjusters who often find themselves in the field, ensuring they have the resources they need right at their fingertips.

BEYOND TECHNOLOGY: THE HUMAN TOUCH

While technology can vastly improve efficiency and productivity, the heart of your firm remains its people. Balancing technological advancements with the personal, empathetic touch that defines your service is key. Use technology to enhance your service, but remember, it's the human connection that truly makes a difference in the lives of those you help.

Incorporating efficient claim management systems and productivity tools is a strategic move that sets your public insurance adjusting firm apart in a competitive industry. It not only streamlines your operations but also empowers your team to focus on what they do best—advocating for clients with expertise, compassion, and dedication. As you embark on this journey of technological integration, keep in mind that the ultimate goal is to enhance your firm's ability to serve your clients efficiently and effectively, building a legacy of excellence and trust.

Outsource and Freelance Options

When each claim is a unique puzzle to solve, the strategic use of outsourcing and engaging freelancers can be akin to bringing in specialized puzzle-solvers. These experts can help manage workload spikes, bring in fresh perspectives, and enhance the firm's overall expertise. However, the decision to outsource should be approached with careful consideration, ensuring it aligns with your firm's values and operational goals. Let's navigate through the strategic assessment and implementation of outsourcing in your firm.

In most jurisdictions, the profession of public adjusting is regulated by state insurance departments. These regulations typically specify that only licensed individuals may perform the duties of a public adjuster. Assisting someone who is not licensed in performing these duties can be considered a violation of these regulations.

Utilizing unlicensed staff for tasks that legally require a public adjuster's license can have serious consequences for both the firm and its clients. Beyond risking regulatory violations and substantial fines, this practice may invalidate claim settlements and expose the firm to liability issues. Common missteps include allowing office staff to negotiate with carriers, provide coverage opinions, or discuss settlement terms directly with clients. Even seemingly routine activities like explaining policy provisions or advising on claim documentation can cross into licensed territory. To protect your firm and ensure compliance, it's crucial to clearly define role boundaries and ensure that all client-facing claim adjustment activities are handled exclusively by licensed professionals.

It is important to distinguish outsourcing which is permissible. It is crucial for public adjusters to ensure that all individuals involved in handling claims on their behalf are properly licensed and qualified for the tasks they are performing.

Identifying Tasks Suitable for Outsourcing

Begin by charting out the landscape of your firm's operations to pinpoint tasks that are prime candidates for outsourcing. Look beyond the surface to identify tasks that, while necessary, might be diverting your core team's attention from their primary responsibilities. This could range from administrative duties that eat into valuable time, to specialized claim analysis that requires niche expertise not currently housed within your firm. The aim is to strategically allocate your internal resources where they can deliver the most value.

Conducting a Cost-Benefit Analysis

Embarking on the outsourcing journey without a map can lead you astray. A detailed cost-benefit analysis acts as this map, helping you weigh the financial outlay of outsourcing against the potential gains in efficiency, productivity, and client satisfaction. Consider not just the immediate costs but also the long-term benefits, such as the potential for scaling your operations more flexibly or enhancing your service quality with specialized expertise.

Seeking Out the Right Partners

The search for the right outsourcing partners is a quest for allies who understand the terrain of public insurance adjusting and share your commitment to excellence. This journey involves:

◆ **Vetting for Expertise and Alignment**

Dive deep into potential partners' backgrounds to ensure they not only have the requisite skills but also align with your firm's ethical standards and dedication to client advocacy.

◆ **Leveraging Networks for Trusted Referrals**

Sometimes, the best paths are those recommended by trusted colleagues. Utilize your professional network to find outsourcing partners who come with stamps of approval.

◆ **Ensuring Compatibility**

Beyond technical skills, seek partners who understand the nuances of your work and can seamlessly integrate into your operational flow, enhancing rather than disrupting your processes.

CRAFTING SUCCESSFUL COLLABORATIONS

Once you've identified potential partners, setting the foundation for a successful collaboration is key. This involves:

Clarifying Expectations and Goals

Establish clear benchmarks and deliverables from the outset. This clarity helps prevent misunderstandings and sets the stage for a productive partnership.

Keeping Communication Channels Open

Regular check-ins and updates ensure that both parties are

aligned and can quickly address any issues or adjustments needed. Think of it as maintaining open lines of navigation to ensure smooth sailing.

Evaluating Performance and Fit

Regular assessments of the outsourcing arrangement help ensure that it continues to meet your firm's needs and contributes positively to your operations.

Understanding the Broader Impact

Outsourcing decisions ripple through your firm, affecting team dynamics, client experiences, and your firm's reputation. It's crucial to:

Communicate with Your Team

Ensure your internal team understands the rationale behind outsourcing decisions and sees them as enhancements to their own work, not replacements.

Monitor Client Impact

Keep a close eye on client feedback and satisfaction to ensure that the quality of service remains high and consistent with your firm's standards.

Stay Flexible and Responsive

The business landscape and your firm's needs will evolve. Maintain flexibility in your outsourcing arrangements to adapt to changing demands and opportunities.

LOOKING AHEAD: OUTSOURCING AS A STRATEGIC TOOL

View outsourcing not merely as a solution to immediate needs but as a strategic tool in your firm's arsenal. It offers a way to dynamically scale your operations, access specialized skills, and even explore new services or markets with minimized risk. By carefully selecting the right tasks to outsource, partnering with the right freelancers or agencies, and integrating them effectively into your operations, you can enhance your firm's agility, efficiency, and competitive edge.

In the business of public adjusting, where each client's needs are as unique as the claims they bring, the judicious use of outsourcing can be a pivotal strategy in delivering unparalleled service. It's about extending the reach of your firm's expertise and capacity, ensuring that you can meet and exceed your clients' expectations, no matter the complexity of the challenge at hand. Remember, in this journey, the goal is not just to manage workload but to enrich your firm's capabilities and solidify its reputation as a leader in the field of public insurance adjusting.

BUILD A POSITIVE AND SUPPORTIVE WORK CULTURE

When the stakes are high and the challenges complex, the importance of nurturing a culture of trust and respect cannot be overstated. It's about creating an environment that not only supports but also empowers every team member to bring their best selves to work. Fostering a work culture that is the bedrock of a thriving, successful firm.

Leaders are the architects of their organizations' cultures. How they behave, communicate, and make decisions sets a standard for others to follow. In the context of a public adjuster who heads an organization, this means leading by example in integrity, dedication, and fairness—qualities essential in the insurance adjusting field. Such leadership ensures that ethical practices are at the core of organizational operations and client interactions.

Liz Wiseman's book *Multipliers* teaches that the best leaders are not just authority figures but facilitators who amplify the intelligence and capabilities of their teams. A public adjuster leading an organization should harness not only their deep expertise in insurance claims adjustment but also their ability to be accessible to others on the team. By being approachable, they encourage open communication, leading to a more collaborative and inclusive work environment.

The concept of a "ripple effect" in leadership is powerful. When leaders act as "multipliers," they enhance the capabilities of their employees. For a public adjuster at the helm, empowering their team can lead to more effective handling of claims, innovative problem-solving, and enhanced client satisfaction. Each team member feels valued and capable, leading to increased productivity and morale.

RICH'S STORY

BUILD YOUR CLAIM HANDLING AND OFFICE SUPPORT TEAM

Rich's journey into team building began with a crucial realization: he couldn't sustainably grow his business while handling every aspect alone. This epiphany led him to strategically break down his responsibilities into distinct roles, each crucial for the smooth operation of his public adjusting firm.

Initially, Rich faced challenges in hiring. His first attempts resulted in a few mismatches — employees who, while qualified on paper, didn't align with his vision or work ethic. These experiences taught Rich the importance of not just skills, but cultural fit and shared values in team members.

Through a process of trial and error, Rich refined his hiring approach. He began to look beyond resumes, focusing on candidates who demonstrated passion for helping others and a commitment to ethical practices. He developed a knack for identifying individuals who could empathize with clients while maintaining professional boundaries.

Rich's perseverance paid off as he gradually assembled a team that aligned perfectly with his goals and values. He hired a detail-oriented office manager to streamline administrative tasks, a tech-savvy claims processor to handle documentation, and empathetic client liaisons to maintain strong relationships with policyholders.

The implementation of ClaimWizard proved to be a game-changer for Rich's team. The software's comprehensive features allowed for seamless collaboration, efficient claim tracking, and improved communication. Rich found that ClaimWizard not only enhanced his team's productivity but also enabled them to provide an even higher level of service to clients.

With his dream team in place and supported by cutting-edge technology, Rich felt a renewed sense of purpose and excitement for the future of his business. He had created not just a company, but a cohesive unit dedicated to excellence in public adjusting.

PART FOUR

CLAIM HANDLING DEEP DIVE

CHAPTER 10
CLAIMS HANDLING AND NEGOTIATION PROCESSES

> Negotiation is the art of letting them have your way.
>
> DANIEL VARE

CREATING an effective workflow for assessing damages, valuing claims, and challenging insurance companies stands as the foundation of the public adjusting field, essential for policyholders facing the challenges of loss. This chapter delves deep into the methodologies, tools and strategies that are crucial for navigating the complexities of the process, transforming them into a system that is both rigorous and transparent. It explores the importance of cutting-edge technology to enhance the accuracy of claim valuations and speed of indemnification.

This narrative goes beyond mere numbers, focusing on ensuring that policyholders receive the support and compensation they are entitled to, facilitating not just the repair of their property but also the recovery of their lives or businesses.

A process is a series of steps for your team to follow. Steps are combined into different collections called "workflows." Each step is a task to be completed by a specific team member or department. In ClaimWizard, these steps are called "Action Items." Creating workflows is a critical prerequisite to success.

If you are not using ClaimWizard for a claim management solution, you can document your workflow on a spreadsheet or flowchart and distribute it to your team. Many benefits of using the ClaimWizard platform will not be available, such as automatic documentation, accountability, escalation, reminders, deadline tracking, and next steps. You will also not be able to export the entire workflow progress of a claim with the click of a button (yes, ClaimWizard is THAT EASY to export claim information to turn over to your legal team, vendor, client, or carrier.)

WHAT ARE WORKFLOWS AND ACTION ITEMS?

ClaimWizard uses Workflows and Action Items to implement an automated, cohesive group of tasks (called a "workflow") related to processing an insurance claim. Action Items and Workflows are unique in the public adjusting industry and pioneered by ClaimWizard.

How to start capturing your workflow

First, you need to document how your company currently adjusts claims. Using a whiteboard, flowchart software, index cards, or even good ol' sticky notes on a big blank wall, let's walk through the process of working a claim. Be sure to document the following for each task:

- Who is responsible for the task
- What part of the claim lifecycle (phase) this task belongs to
- What is this task dependent on
- What happens when this task is overdue

- What happens when this task is completed
- How long this task should take to complete

Some tasks can be worked on simultaneously with others, and some have hard dependencies. Document it all.

Note that an Action Item is not giving the nitty-gritty details of how to perform a task (such as explicitly explaining *how* to perform a contents inventory) but rather frame-working the task and the parameters in which it is considered complete.

Next, think about any 'exception phases' a claim may encounter. Pre/Litigation, Mediation, Re-Inspection, Appraisal, etc., are possible unexpected turns in a claim. Document your preferred business process for dealing with each of these exemption claim phases (using a different color marker or index card for each exception type is helpful.)

In ClaimWizard, these sets of Action Items stay dormant until there is a specific need to invoke them within the lifecycle of a claim. This approach helps your entire team stick to a pre-approved path when working with situations that may not be 'top of mind.' We will be working through Exception Phase Action Items in the next section.

If your company uses ClaimWizard, you can quickly enter your Action Items directly from your worksheet or flowchart.

Whether you are a single public adjuster business or a multi-national public adjusting company, ClaimWizard Action Item Workflows will make your claim adjusting process more time-efficient, thus, more profitable.

After brainstorming all possible tasks required to compete a claim, group your tasks in the rough order they should be executed. Every claim can be bucketed into four major parts:

1. Claim Origination and Onboarding
2. Estimating and Adjusting
3. Post-Determination

4. Financial and Compliance Reconciliation

ORIGINATION & ONBOARDING	ESTIMATING & ADJUSTMENT	POST-DETERMINATION	FINANCIAL & COMPLIANCE RECONCILIATION
Initial acquisition and intake of the claim, including gathering loss documentation, signing representation agreements, and establishing the claim file with required permissions and paperwork.	Creation of detailed damage assessments and loss estimates, followed by negotiations with the insurance carrier's adjuster to establish a fair settlement value.	Review and response to the carrier's settlement offer, including acceptance or preparation of supplemental documentation to support additional claimed damages.	Final phase ensuring proper payment distribution and documentation completion while maintaining regulatory compliance and fulfilling contractual obligations.

CLAIM ORIGINATION AND ONBOARDING

The claim journey begins here — a critical first step where the policyholder's claim is officially registered with the insurance carrier and information about the loss is gathered. This phase is about establishing a solid foundation for the claim by:

Client Contract

Every claim you handle begins with a signed client contract. This contract is signed by the policyholder authorizing the public adjuster to act on their behalf. This form should also specify the fees due to the public adjuster by the policyholder, authorization to negotiate the claim and receive claim-related information and endorsing settlement checks. It is typical that you will have a unique Client Contract for each state you operate in. State level Department of Insurance approval of your contract is required. If you need assistance with designing these contracts, Holly Soffer of Kellis Soffer, LLC (https://kellissoffer.com) is our #1 choice in legal professionals. She has a deep understanding of not only the public adjusting space, but of state insurance laws and requirements.

While a claim may start for your company with a signed

client contract, the insurance carrier needs to be legally notified of your involvement. This document — sometimes referred to as a Letter of Representation (LOR), Letter of Notice (LON), or Letter of Intent (LOI) — clearly states your authority to represent the policyholder. It must include the public adjuster's contact information, license number, the policyholder's full name and policy number, the address of the property where losses took place, and the type of peril that occurred. In ClaimWizard, generating this document is as easy as clicking a button.

Request for Information (RFI)

This is the opportune time to request a certified copy of the insurance policy and declaration page in-force at the time of loss. Be sure to review the policy declarations and forms schedule and compare it to the policy pages you are provided. If the policyholder has already initiated the claim process, requesting any correspondence (emails, letters, loss documentation, denial letters, etc.) from the insurance carrier can help maintain continuity and transparency.

Client Welcome Communication

As we've covered many times — and will continue to stress — open, timely, and clear communication with your client is imperative. Use this opportunity to construct a Welcome Letter (or email) to your client that gives them an overview of the process you will take to settle their claim. Include items such as:

1. A sincere "thank you" for their business and trust
2. Signed copy of the contract between you and client
3. If using ClaimWizard: Link to Client Portal and login credentials
4. Your company's W-9 form
5. IINK finance flyer or mortgage authorization form for client to complete and return to you

6. Letter of Representation for client to complete and return to you (sometimes this is completed when you have your client sign your contract)
7. Fee payment policies
8. Frequently asked questions
9. Public adjuster and company contact information (should they call or email their adjuster or office, etc.)
10. Next steps such as "notice given to insurance company," "schedule on-site inspection," etc.

We strongly advise against giving exact timeframes or dates, outside of when you need initial documentation signed and returned to you.

ESTIMATING AND ADJUSTING

Here, as the Wizards say, is where the magic happens. The estimation and adjustment process is at the heart of a component of a public adjusting company's workflow. Here's a typical process that public adjusting companies follow:

Initial Assessment and Adjustment

The public adjuster visits the site of the damage to conduct a thorough inspection. This involves taking photographs, making notes, and sometimes using technology like drones for hard-to-reach areas or 3D imaging for internal structures.

Document Review

If not done prior, the public adjuster reviews the insurance policy in detail to understand the coverage, limitations, and exclusions. This helps in determining what damages are covered under the policy.

Damage Assessment

The public adjuster assesses the extent of the damage, which may involve consulting with specialists like structural engineers, roofers, or water restoration experts to understand the full scope of the damage.

ESTIMATION PROCESS

Re-Construction Cost Estimation

Utilizing specialized software (like Xactimate), the public adjuster prepares an itemized estimate of the repair costs. This includes materials, labor, and other expenses necessary to restore the property to its pre-loss condition.

Content Inventory

If property within a structure is damaged, the adjuster will create a detailed inventory list, noting the age, value, photographs if available, receipts, and replacement cost of each item. Content is usually considered as anything that would fall out of a building if you shook the structure upside down, but of course check the specific policy for details.

Additional Living Expenses or Business Interruption

Additional Living Expenses (ALE) and Business Interruption (BI) insurance both aim to offset financial losses from disruptions, targeting distinct groups. ALE helps individuals with extra costs when displaced from their homes by disasters, ensuring their living standards are maintained during repairs. BI protects businesses from losses caused by temporary closures or reduced operations, covering lost income and expenses to maintain financial stability and aid in recovery.

Negotiation

Negotiating with an insurance company is a pivotal aspect of a public adjuster's role, providing substantial value to policyholders during the claims process. This negotiation process involves several key steps and strategies aimed at ensuring the policyholder receives a fair and just settlement in line with the policy's coverage. Here's an overview of the process and its inherent value:

Initial Claim Submission

The adjuster submits the detailed claim report to the insurance carrier, including the estimate, content inventory pricing list, and any additional documentation that will support your case. This is the step in the claims process where a Proof of Loss (POL) may come into play.

A Proof of Loss is a formal document a policyholder must submit to an insurance company to document a claim's specifics and request reimbursement for a loss. It is a critical step in the insurance claims process, particularly for property and casualty insurance. This document typically includes the following key elements:

- Date of Loss: Specifies when the damage or loss occurred.
- Type of Loss: Describes the nature of the event that caused the damage (e.g., fire, flood, theft).
- Location of Loss: Indicates where the damage occurred.
- Amount of Loss Claimed: Details the monetary value of the loss, supported by estimates, invoices, and other documentation that justifies the claimed amount.
- Policy Number: Identifies the insurance policy under which the claim is made.
- Claim Number: If provided by the insurance company upon initial claim reporting, this helps in tracking and referencing the claim.
- Documentation of Damage: May include photos, repair estimates, receipts for expenses incurred, and any other evidence that supports the claim.

The Proof of Loss must be signed by the policyholder, often under oath, affirming the accuracy of the information provided.

In this structure it is referred to as a Sworn Proof of Loss (SPOL.) This document serves several purposes: it formally notifies the insurance company of the claim, provides a basis for assessing the claim's validity, and outlines the financial impact of the loss on the policyholder.

Insurance policies usually specify a timeframe within which the Proof of Loss must be submitted following a loss, and failing to meet this deadline can jeopardize the claim. Once submitted, the insurance company reviews the Proof of Loss as part of its claim evaluation process to decide on claim approval and the amount of settlement.

Be sure to review not only the policy you are working with but any state insurance regulations surrounding this step. Many states have deadlines associated with submitting a POL that you must adhere to in order to stay compliant with the law.

Initial Carrier Review

The insurance company's adjuster reviews the submitted claim and may conduct their own assessment. They might agree with the public adjuster's findings or propose adjustments.

NEGOTIATIONS

If there are discrepancies between the public adjuster's estimates and the insurance company's figures (*and there **always** are…*), negotiations ensue. The public adjuster advocates for the policyholder, aiming to reach an agreement that accurately reflects the cost of repairs and replacements.

The Value of Negotiation

This is *the thing* you are paid to do. Prove, determine policy coverage, and price damage indemnification for policyholders. If you are looking to add to your Unique Selling Proposition (see Chapter 4), these are what you will want to focus on:

- Maximizing Claim Value: Public adjusters leverage their expertise to ensure that all aspects of the claim are accurately assessed and fully compensated, often identifying damages or coverages that the policyholder may not have been aware of.
- Expertise and Experience: Public adjusters bring a deep understanding of insurance policies and the claims process, enabling them to effectively counter lowball offers or incorrect interpretations of policy language by the insurer.
- Efficient Resolution: Skilled in negotiation tactics, public adjusters can often expedite the settlement process, avoiding delays and getting policyholders the funds they need more quickly.
- Reducing Stress: Handling insurance claims can be overwhelming for policyholders. Public adjusters take on the burden of negotiation, allowing policyholders to focus on recovery and rebuilding.
- Advocacy: Public adjusters serve as dedicated advocates for the policyholder, representing their interests alone. This contrasts with insurance company adjusters, who aim to minimize the company's payouts.

In essence, the negotiation process conducted by public adjusters is invaluable for policyholders, not only in terms of potentially increasing the settlement amount but also in navigating the complexities of insurance claims with confidence and support. Public adjusters' skills and persistence in negotiation can make a significant difference in the outcome of a claim, ensuring policyholders receive fair treatment and just compensation.

POST-DETERMINATION

This phase, Post-Carrier Determination, involves the resolution of the claim following the insurance carrier's decision. Let's not gloss over this step, as it rarely happens easily or quickly. While represented in just one section here, in actuality this is the most grueling aspect of a claim. This stage focuses on:

Reviewing the Carrier Settlement Offer

Carefully examining the insurance company's offer to ensure it aligns with the policy terms and adequately covers the damages. If not, you are now entering the following…

Exception Phases

If necessary, you will not "move directly to GO and collect $200," but rather embark in a "choose your own adventure" scenario determinate on the carrier's determination. Since these are fairly typical paths of non-indemnification from an insurance carrier, you should have your processes pre-built for these situations.

In the context of property insurance claims, several situations can arise that necessitate specific actions or processes. Understanding these terms and their implications can help policyholders navigate the complexities of filing and resolving a claim.

Here's an overview of each term in the context of property insurance claims:

◆ Re-Inspection

A re-inspection occurs when there is a need to reassess the property damage after the initial inspection. This can be requested by the insurance company, the policyholder, or a public adjuster if there are discrepancies in the damage assessment, if additional damages are discovered, or if repairs have been completed and need verification. Re-inspections can lead to adjustments in the claim amount. They are crucial for ensuring that all damages are accurately documented and compensated.

◆ **Coverage Dispute**

A coverage dispute arises when there is a disagreement between the policyholder and the insurance company over what is covered under the policy terms. This can involve interpretations of policy language regarding exclusions, limits, or conditions. Resolving coverage disputes may require negotiation, mediation, or, in some cases, legal intervention. It's essential for policyholders to understand their policy thoroughly and seek professional advice if needed.

◆ **Appraisal**

The appraisal process is a method used to resolve disputes about the value of the property damage claim. When the policyholder and insurer cannot agree on the amount of the loss, each party selects an independent appraiser. The two appraisers then select an umpire, and an agreement by any two of these three resolves the dispute. Appraisal can be a faster, less costly alternative to litigation and helps both parties reach a fair settlement based on the damage valuation.

◆ **Partial Denials**

Partial denials occur when an insurance company agrees to cover some, but not all, of a claim. This can happen when certain damages are deemed not covered under the policy or exceed the policy limits. Policyholders receiving partial denials must decide whether to accept the decision and cover the remaining costs out-of-pocket, or to dispute the denial through appeals, appraisal, or litigation.

◆ **Pre-Litigation**

Pre-litigation refers to the actions and negotiations that take place before formally filing a lawsuit if a claim cannot be settled through the usual process of adjustment. Litigation comes into play when these disputes cannot be resolved, leading to a legal case where a court decides on the matter. Litigation can be time-consuming and costly, so it's often considered a last resort. Pre-litigation efforts aim to resolve disputes amicably and avoid court.

Each of these scenarios requires careful documentation and often legal advice. Public adjusters facing these situations should consider consulting with a legal professional to ensure their client's rights are protected and to maximize their claim settlement. Public adjusters should be careful not to provide legal opinions which indicate the best course of action or apply facts to law to make such opinions which are then offered to the policyholder.

FINANCIAL AND COMPLIANCE RECONCILIATION

Once a satisfactory settlement is reached, guiding the policyholder through the process of receiving their compensation and beginning the restoration or repair work. This step also includes providing advice on preventing future losses and possibly reviewing and updating the insurance policy to reflect any new risks or changes in property value.

Claim Payment and Company Fee Distribution

In the context of a public adjusting company, managing claim payments and the disbursement of company fees is a critical aspect of operations. These processes involve the flow of funds from insurance companies to policyholders and from policyholders to the public adjusting company as compensation for services rendered.

Once an insurance claim has been settled and the insurance company agrees to pay, the process for disbursing those funds begins. The specifics can vary depending on the insurance policy, the nature of the claim, and state regulations, but generally, the steps are as follows:

Issuance of Payment

The insurance company issues payment for the agreed-upon

claim amount. This payment can be made directly to the policyholder or, in cases where a public adjuster is involved and with the policyholder's authorization, directly to the public adjusting company.

Allocation for Repairs and Recovery

The funds are intended to cover repair costs, replace lost or damaged property, or compensate for losses as specified in the claim settlement. Policyholders are responsible for allocating these funds appropriately to cover the costs of their loss recovery.

Public Adjuster Company Fee Disbursement

Public adjusting companies earn their fees based on a percentage of the claim settlement, a flat fee, or a combination of these structures, as agreed upon in their contract with the policyholder. The process for disbursing these fees involves:

Calculation of Fees

Once the claim payment is received, the public adjusting company calculates its fees based on the agreed-upon rate and the total settlement amount.

Invoice and Payment

The public adjusting company then issues an invoice to the policyholder for their services. If the insurance payment was made directly to the public adjusting company, the firm deducts its fees and disburses the remaining funds to the policyholder. If the payment was made directly to the policyholder, they are responsible for paying the public adjuster's invoice from those funds. Chances are carrier payment checks will trickle in and need to be distributed accordingly. This is absolutely where we recommend using a financial services like IINK to not only handle check processing but mortgage handling (multi-party checks.)

Internal Company Disbursement

Once the company fee is collected, it still typically needs to be broken down further to pay adjusters, vendors, and any other party that receives compensation from a claim. Chapter 3 outlines what your potential costs and percentages are.

KEY CONSIDERATIONS

Compliance and Ethics

Public adjusting companies must comply with state regulations governing insurance claims and public adjuster fees. Ethical practices in fee calculation and disbursement are crucial for preserving the integrity of the profession.

Documentation

Both the claim payment process and the fee disbursement process should be well-documented. This includes maintaining records of all communications, invoices, and payments related to the claim and the public adjuster's services.

Managing claim payments and fee disbursement efficiently and ethically is fundamental to the operation of a public adjusting company. It ensures that policyholders receive the funds necessary to recover from their loss and that the public adjusting firm is compensated fairly for its expertise and services.

THE CLAIM CLOSING PROCESS

The claim closing process should be part of your overall claim workflow. Remember, it doesn't have to be an overbearing process that takes a lot of time. This can be a basic form that is included in the claim's folder or file repository.

- The compliance questions must be reviewed for every single claim.
- The financial questions should be reviewed on a regular basis.

- The relationship questions should also be reviewed frequently.
- The customer survey should be conducted every time.

Your closing process should also include a checklist to ensure final details haven't been overlooked. Some sample checklist items might include:

- Were all disbursements paid?
- Are any holdbacks or supplemental adjustments or payments due?
- If co-endorsement was required, were all payments collected? Were fees and disbursements in compliance with state limits? Did the contract accurately reflect the company fee?
- Were all contracts signed by the appropriate parties?
- If the company fee changed, was the contract amended? Were your fees collected?
- Were commissions paid to your staff, partners, and vendors?
- Your closing process should also include a formal archival method, preferably off-site, backed up, and cloud-based.
- Depending on the state where the loss occurred as well as your own state of operation, the statute requires archiving AND retrieval for 3-7 years. Materials should include issuance, tracking, collection, recording, and surveys.
- If CWP (closed without pay), did you thoroughly document the reason for the closure?
- If canceled, have you protected yourself through supporting documentation?

NAVIGATING THE CLAIMS PROCESS EFFICIENTLY AND EFFECTIVELY

Having an easy-to-follow, documented, repeatable, and automated business process to adjust claims from claim origination to adjuster fee disbursement is critical to keeping your public adjusting business compliant, efficient, and profitable.

Additional Benefits of Workflows

Besides the structure and order workflows created in your business, several other benefits come with designing and implementing a workflow for your public adjusting business. These include:

- Insight into your unique business process,
- Identifying redundancies,
- Increased accountability and reduced micromanagement,
- Improved communication and documentation,
- Better customer service,
- Improved quality and speed of services, and
- Ease of updating procedures to comply with law changes.

Let's look at each one more closely.

◆ INSIGHT INTO YOUR UNIQUE BUSINESS PROCESSES

Mapping out your processes in a workflow allows you to get a more precise, top-level view of your adjusting business. Even if you have a well-established set of tasks and deadlines to settle a claim, do you know if they are working as efficiently as they can be? Are there unnecessary redundancies? Are they taking too long to complete? How about documentation? What processes need more time and attention to detail, and which ones can be automated? Can you easily compile the necessary documentation quickly and accurately if the claim goes to litigation?

One of the biggest reasons workflow is essential is that it gives you greater insight into your entire business. From then on, you can use these insights to better your workflows and improve the bottom line of your business: *sign and close more claims faster and make more profit.*

◆ **Identify Redundancies**

In most businesses, many unnecessary and redundant tasks occur over the lifecycle of a claim; this is especially true within public adjusting. Team members can be performing functions at the wrong time, duplicating work efforts, or skipping essential duties altogether. Once you have your adjusting process documented, you can determine what activities are crucial.

Identifying and eliminating redundant tasks has countless benefits — it creates value, saves time, and saves money for your business. Instead of wasting time on useless tasks, your team will be able to focus on what's important and what does contribute to the successful and profitable settlement of claims.

◆ **Increased Accountability and Reduced Micromanagement**

Micromanagement can cause many problems in a business setting: staff hate micromanagers, and (most) owners/managers hate having to do it.

However, there might not be any other solution but micromanagement in some cases. There's vital work to be done, and not everyone is as motivated to do it. Just because tasks need to be done — and done on time — doesn't mean that YOU are the one that needs to stand over your staff's shoulders and babysit. The best solution is to provide a clearly defined workflow that allows you to delegate to your team — including task deadlines, next steps, and escalation paths. (Using ClaimWizard, this can all happen automatically without your direct involvement.)

When a workflow process is laid out in this way, you can spend less time micromanaging staff. There's no questioning what the further steps are needed or if "08. Send Proof of Loss to Carrier" is overdue. Everyone on the team sees exactly what's going on and what needs to get done, and by whom. Knowing that you can count on your team to understand what they should be doing next and having the accountability to confirm the work is being done makes it easier to trust your team. This helps to reduce the need for micromanagement, which is also a symptom of a lack of trust.

This will, in turn, increase the job satisfaction of everyone involved and will most likely improve the relationships between ownership and staff — and, most importantly, between your company and your clients.

◆ **Improved Communication and Documentation**

Have you ever felt your office is like a game of telephone? Everyone is talking, but somewhere along the way, the message becomes garbled. Nothing is documented in the same way across member's of your staff. Poor client communication can lead to canceled contracts, costly misunderstandings, or worse.

This leads us to another big reason why workflow is essential: the visibility of processes and accountability can increase communication dramatically and improve client trust. Not to mention that taking a claim to litigation becomes as easy as clicking a few buttons to generate a complete set of discoverable documents. This includes a full accounting of every task that has been performed.

A further perk of improved communication and documentation can reduce staff turnover, onboard new staff faster, and make day-to-day operations smoother overall.

◆ **Better Customer Service**

Without your customers, there is no business to run. So, it is essential to find ways to improve the customer experience continually, ideally with a minimum impact on your staff.

Unfortunately, customer requests or complaints can be easily overlooked when relying on pen and paper to document and escalate issues. With ClaimWizard, we help you identify issues before they become problems.

However, when an issue does arise, Action Items make it easy to track and resolve.

Sloppy or inconsistent communication can result in dissatisfied clients. The easiest way to counter this is to include clients in the adjusting process at the appropriate milestones — and communicate those processes with them. Consider including an abbreviated and client-friend version of your process in your Client Welcome letter. This way, clients know what to expect at every step of the claim process.

◆ **Improved Quality and Speed of Your Services**

Often, team members are assigned tasks based on who is available rather than who has the best skill set to perform that job. Another reason why going through the process of designing a claim process workflow is essential it allows you to think about and select the team member/role who is best suited to perform the available tasks. For example, office staff might be better to contact clients and carriers to coordinate an on-property inspection than your Public Adjuster. Every minute a Public Adjuster is spending on the phone or waiting for a callback is a minute they aren't performing their two core initiatives: sign more business and adjust more claims.

By automating workflows, you can reduce the likelihood of human error, missed communication, or incomplete documentation.

◆ **Ease of Updating Procedures to Comply with Law Changes**

When it comes to Public Adjusting companies, staying on the right side of the law is crucial. That's where a documented and automated workflow plan comes into play to ensure legal compliance.

Having a documented workflow plan brings consistency and standardization to how the company — and individual team members — handle insurance claims. It lays out the steps, procedures, and guidelines that employees should follow. Most importantly, when laws change, processes can be updated immediately so that team members do not have the burden of translating the law updates to the claim workflow. This consistency reduces the chances of mistakes or omissions that could lead to legal trouble.

DESIGN A PROCESS THAT WORKS FOR YOUR COMPANY

It's important to remember that the role of ownership/management in any company is that of leadership and motivation. You have to help your staff cross bridges. Some of them will freeze part of the way across (and refuse to go any further), and some will run full speed ahead (missing critical tasks along the way.) Both can be hazardous to your company process.

Leadership needs to help them get used to using new ways of doing their job and help them understand how it's used and the value in it. Every team member will benefit from a tool like Workflows in ClaimWizard, so "selling" them on it is the best approach.

This is a lesson often taught to salespeople: customers don't care about your products or company; they care about the benefits and how it will impact them. "What's In It For ME?" You sell the benefits, not the product when you want to sell something. You aren't selling clients a "document generation, signing, and mailing service," you are selling people who have suffered a loss to their property a means to rebuild by collecting monies for damages that are rightfully and legally theirs.

When you "sell" a new business process to your team, you need to show them the benefits. This includes the time savings, efficiency, accountability, and precision that a well-designed business process can provide them. Answer their question, "What's in it for me?"

Suppose you force new process management tools on your staff members without explaining the "why" or the benefits. In that case, you'll likely experience a lot more pushback and abandonment of your initiative.

Staff needs to understand why the new technology is an improvement, the benefits of using it, and how it will impact the work they perform within the company.

In the end, *you* set the rules of how your company is run.

RICH'S STORY

CLAIMS HANDLING AND NEGOTIATION SPROCESSES

As Rich's public adjusting business grew, he initially approached each claim as a unique project, meticulously crafting individualized strategies for every case. While this attention to detail was admirable, it often led to inefficiencies and occasional oversights, especially as the volume of claims increased.

However, as Rich gained more experience, he began to notice recurring patterns across different claims. Despite the unique circumstances of each case, he realized that there was a common thread of steps and deadlines that applied universally. This revelation prompted Rich to step back and analyze his approach more systematically.

Rich set about designing a comprehensive workflow process for claims handling. He mapped out the typical lifecycle of a claim, identifying key milestones, common pitfalls, and critical deadlines. This structured approach allowed him to create a standardized procedure that could be applied to various types of claims while still allowing for customization where necessary.

Implementing this new workflow was transformative. Legal deadlines, which had previously been a source of stress, became manageable milestones within the larger process. Rich found that by having a clear, step-by-step procedure, his team could work more efficiently and with greater confidence.

Communicating the importance of this new system to his team was crucial. Rich held several training sessions, emphasizing how following the procedure would not only streamline their work but also ensure better outcomes for their clients. He stressed the importance of each team member understanding their role and responsibilities within the larger process.

As the team adapted to the new workflow, Rich noticed a significant improvement in their efficiency and accuracy. Claims were processed more swiftly, deadlines were consistently met, and clients reported higher satisfaction. Rich's systematic approach had transformed his business, proving that while each claim was unique, a well-designed process could effectively handle them all.

CHAPTER 11
MANAGING CLIENT EXPECTATIONS

> The key is to set realistic customer expectations, and then not to just meet them, but to exceed them — preferably in unexpected and helpful ways.
>
> RICHARD BRANSON

IN THE INTRICATE realm of public insurance adjusting, mastering the art of managing client expectations is not merely a professional necessity; it is akin to a sorcerer's craft, weaving a spell of trust and understanding. This nuanced skill demands not only technical expertise but also a profound comprehension of human nature and the diverse spectrum of policyholder profiles. Each client brings a unique set of expectations, capacities, and levels of sophistication, making your role as an adjuster both challenging and vital.

Policyholders vary significantly, ranging from individuals dealing with residential losses to entities grappling with large-scale commercial or governmental claims. This diversity necessitates a tailored approach for each case. Residential clients often require more guidance and emotional support, as they may be navigating the claims process for the first time under stressful circumstances. In contrast, commercial and governmental clients typically possess a higher degree of sophistication regarding insurance matters but still require clear, strategic guidance to navigate the complexities of large-scale claims.

The human and emotional elements are paramount in this process. For many policyholders, especially in residential cases, an insurance claim is not just a financial transaction but a path to recovery from a personal loss. Recognizing and addressing these emotional undercurrents is crucial. The public adjuster must transcend the role of a mere facilitator of claims; they must become a trusted advisor and advocate, a beacon of hope in a policyholder's time of need.

This chapter aims to illuminate the strategies and practices essential for managing a diverse array of client expectations. By emphasizing empathy, clear communication, and a personalized approach, public adjusters can effectively navigate the multifaceted landscape of insurance claims. The goal is to ensure every policyholder, regardless of their claim's nature or their personal experience with insurance, to view their public adjuster as a steadfast ally in their journey towards a fair and just resolution.

SET CLEAR EXPECTATIONS WITH CLIENTS FROM THE BEGINNING

Foundation of Trust

The initial consultation serves as the bedrock of the client-adjuster relationship. This pivotal meeting is more than a mere exchange of information; it is a unique opportunity to establish a bond of trust and set the tone for all future interactions. The adjuster's ability to listen attentively, demonstrate empathy, and show genuine concern for the client's situation plays a critical role in building this foundation. It is during this initial encounter that the client begins to develop confidence in the adjuster's expertise and commitment to their case.

Information Gathering

A thorough understanding of the client's claim and personal needs is paramount in this phase. This step involves a meticulous review of the claim details, including a full examination of the entire policy coverage provisions (RTFP—Read The Full Policy), the nature of the loss, and any pertinent documentation. It's also a time to understand the client's personal circumstances and how the loss has impacted them. This comprehensive approach ensures the adjuster fully grasps the scope of the claim and the client's expectations, allowing for a more tailored and effective handling of the case.

Realistic Outlook

Establishing realistic expectations from the outset is crucial to the success of the claims process. This involves providing the client with a clear and honest overview of potential timelines, the steps involved in the claims process, and the possible outcomes. The adjuster should discuss the complexities and challenges that might arise, such as issues with policy interpretations or negotiations with insurance companies. By setting realistic expectations, the adjuster helps to prevent future misunderstandings and frustrations. It is important to balance optimism with practicality, ensuring the client remains hopeful yet prepared for various scenarios.

Educational Approach

Part of setting clear expectations involves educating the client about the claims process. Many clients may not be familiar with the intricacies of insurance policies and the adjuster's role. Providing a basic understanding of these elements empowers clients and helps demystify the process. This educational approach should be tailored to the client's level of knowledge and experience with insurance claims.

Customized Strategy

Each client's situation is unique, and thus, the strategy for handling their claim should be customized. The adjuster should discuss the specific approach they plan to take with the client's claim, explaining the rationale behind each decision and action. The possibility of hiring experts and how they are going to be paid may be discussed as part of that strategy. This personalized strategy not only reinforces the client's trust but also ensures that they are fully aware of how their claim will be managed.

Set Milestones

Part of managing expectations involves setting clear milestones and goals throughout the claims process. This could include timelines for submitting documentation, expected dates for insurance company responses, and potential meetings or negotiations. By outlining these milestones, clients are better prepared for the journey ahead and can measure progress against these benchmarks.

The initial consultation is a multifaceted process that lays the groundwork for a successful client-adjuster relationship. By building trust, thoroughly understanding the client's needs, setting realistic expectations, educating the client, customizing the strategy, and setting clear milestones, public adjusters can effectively manage client expectations from the very beginning. This approach not only facilitates smoother claim handling but also fosters a sense of security and confidence in the client.

PROVIDE TRANSPARENT AND HONEST COMMUNICATION

Acknowledge Limitations

In the intricate dance of managing client expectations, transparency is the lead step. It is vital for public adjusters to openly discuss the complexities and potential hurdles inherent in the claims process. This candid approach involves acknowledging the limitations of what can be achieved, the potential for delays, and the challenges that might arise during negotiations with insurance companies. By setting a realistic framework from the outset, clients are less likely to harbor unrealistic expectations or feel disillusioned as the process unfolds. This transparency not only manages expectations but also builds trust, as clients appreciate the honesty and straightforwardness of their adjuster.

Open Dialogue

Encouraging an open line of communication is essential in fostering a healthy client-adjuster relationship. Clients should feel comfortable voicing their concerns, asking questions, and expressing their needs. This open dialogue creates a collaborative atmosphere where clients feel valued and heard. It's important for adjusters to actively listen, acknowledge the client's concerns, and provide clear and thoughtful responses. This two-way communication ensures clients are kept in the loop and are active participants in the claims process.

Empathetic Responses

Transparency and honesty should be delivered with empathy and understanding. Recognizing the emotional impact of a loss and the stress of the claims process on clients is crucial. Adjusters should strive to communicate in a way that is not only informative but also compassionate and reassuring. This empathetic approach helps in building a strong, trusting relationship with the client.

Feedback Mechanism

Implementing a feedback mechanism where clients can share their thoughts about the process and the service, they are receiving is beneficial. This feedback allows adjusters to modify their approach and communication style to better suit the client's needs and preferences. It also demonstrates to clients that their opinions are valued and considered, further strengthening the relationship.

Providing transparent and honest communication is a

multifaceted approach that involves acknowledging limitations, clarifying roles, encouraging open dialogue, offering consistent updates, responding empathetically, and implementing a feedback mechanism. These practices are instrumental in managing client expectations effectively, building trust, and ensuring a smooth and collaborative claims process.

MANAGE EXPECTATIONS ABOUT CLAIM SETTLEMENT

Educational Approach

An integral part of managing expectations is educating clients about the multifaceted nature of claim settlements. This involves a detailed explanation of how various factors can influence the outcome, including policy limits and sub-limits, potential exclusions, deductibles, the nature and extent of the damage, and the specific terms and conditions of the insurance policy. Clients should be made aware of how these elements interplay to affect the valuation of their claim. Additionally, it's important to educate clients about the typical practices and perspectives of insurance companies, which may differ from those of the policyholder. This knowledge empowers clients to have realistic expectations and a better understanding of the negotiation process.

Outcome Scenarios

Discussing potential outcome scenarios is crucial in setting realistic expectations. This involves walking clients through various possibilities, from the best-case scenario, where the claim is settled amicably and swiftly, to more challenging situations where there might be significant disagreements over the valuation. It's important to prepare clients for the possibility of negotiations and even disputes, explaining that such scenarios are a normal part of the claims process. This helps in tempering their expectations and prepares them for the range of possible outcomes.

Timeframe Transparency

Providing clients with a realistic timeline for the settlement process is essential. This includes discussing the steps involved in the claims process, from the initial filing to the final settlement, and the time each step may take. It's important to highlight that while some claims may be resolved relatively quickly, others, especially those involving substantial disagreements or complex issues, may take longer. Being transparent about the potential for delays helps manage client expectations and reduces frustration.

Response and Objection Handling

Clients should be informed that disagreements and challenges from the insurance company's representatives are common. These challenges may pertain to the public adjuster's valuation and the claimed amount. Educating clients about this aspect of the process is crucial, as it prepares them for the reality that their initial claim may not be accepted without question. It's important to reassure clients that responding to objections and negotiating with insurance companies is a core part of what public adjusters do. This involves a strategic approach to presenting documentation, negotiating amounts of loss, debating coverages, and advocating for the client's best interests.

Negotiation Preparedness

Preparing clients for the negotiation process is a key aspect of managing expectations. This includes discussing strategies for responding to counteroffers, the importance of documentation and evidence in supporting the claim, and the potential need for compromise in some areas. Clients should understand that negotiations are a normal and expected part of reaching a fair settlement and that their public adjuster is equipped with the expertise and experience to navigate these negotiations effectively.

Emphasize Patience and Persistence

Clients should be encouraged to have patience throughout the settlement process. It's important to stress that while the public adjuster will work diligently to expedite the process, some aspects, such as waiting for responses from insurance companies, expert inspections, or scheduling meetings, can take time. Persistence and a steady approach are often key to achieving a favorable outcome.

In summary, managing expectations regarding claim settlement involves an educational approach, discussing outcome scenarios, being transparent about timeframes, preparing clients for responses and objections, emphasizing negotiation preparedness, and encouraging patience and persistence. By setting realistic expectations and preparing clients for the complexities of the settlement process, public adjusters can foster a more informed and less stressful experience for their clients.

EFFECTIVELY COMMUNICATING THROUGHOUT THE CLAIMS PROCESS

Establishing Regular Communication Channels

The foundation of effective communication lies in understanding and adapting to the client's preferred methods of communication. This personalization can significantly enhance the client experience. Whether it's through email, phone calls, text messages, virtual video meetings, or in-person meetings, identifying and using the channels the client is most comfortable with is key. This approach not only ensures the client is more receptive to the information but also demonstrates a commitment to catering to their individual needs.

Update Schedules

Establishing a regular and predictable schedule for updates and progress reports regarding the adjustment is essential in maintaining a transparent and trustful relationship. This schedule should be agreed upon early in the relationship, taking into consideration the complexity of the claim and the client's need for information. Regular updates provide a rhythm to the communication, ensuring the client is consistently informed about the status of their claim and any significant developments. This predictability in communication helps in reducing anxiety and uncertainty for the client.

Accessibility

Ensuring clients can easily reach the adjuster for inquiries is crucial in fostering a sense of reliability and support. This means being responsive to calls, emails, and messages, and providing timely responses. Accessibility also involves being available to address any unexpected concerns or questions that may arise. The adjuster should strive to be as available as possible within reasonable boundaries, as this accessibility greatly contributes to the client feeling supported and valued. The most successful public adjusters provide cell phone numbers to their clients and make themselves available nearly 24/7.

Streamlining Communication

To make the client experience as free of frustration as possible, it's important to streamline communication. This involves organizing and consolidating information in a way that is easy for the client to understand and process. Avoiding overly technical language, being concise, and focusing on key points can make communication more effective. Providing summaries or highlights of complex documents or processes can also be helpful.

Proactive Approach

A proactive communication approach can significantly enhance the client experience. This involves anticipating the client's needs and questions and addressing them before they arise. Providing clients with guides, FAQs, or informational resources at the outset can preempt many common queries and concerns, making the process feel smoother and more manageable for the client.

Feedback Mechanism

Implementing a feedback mechanism where clients can share their thoughts about the communication process is beneficial. This feedback allows the adjuster to modify their communication style and methods to better suit the client's preferences. It also demonstrates to clients that their input is valued and considered further enhancing their experience.

Empathy and Understanding

Throughout all communications, it's important to convey empathy and understanding. Recognizing the emotional impact of the situation on the client and responding with compassion can make a significant difference in their experience. This empathetic approach helps in building a strong, trusting relationship with the client.

Effectively communicating throughout the claims process involves adapting to preferred communication modes, establishing regular update schedules, ensuring accessibility, streamlining communication, taking a proactive approach, implementing a feedback mechanism, and consistently demonstrating empathy and understanding. These practices not only ensure effective and efficient communication but also contribute to making the client's experience with the public adjuster as free of frustration as possible, reinforcing the perception that it is easy and reassuring to do business with the public adjuster.

Emotional Intelligence

The ability to recognize and understand the emotional toll of the claims process on clients is a critical aspect of a public adjuster's role. This emotional intelligence involves acknowledging the stress, anxiety, and sometimes even grief that clients may experience because of their loss and the ensuing claims process. It's important for adjusters to be attuned to these emotional states and respond in a way that shows understanding and sensitivity to the client's situation.

Transparency in Communication

Transparency is key in all communications related to complaint resolution. Clients should be kept informed about the progress of their complaint and any actions being taken. This transparency helps in building trust and demonstrates the adjuster's commitment to resolving the issue.

PROVIDING TIMELY UPDATES AND PROGRESS REPORTS

Status Reports

An essential aspect of maintaining a positive client relationship is the provision of regular status reports. These reports should comprehensively inform clients about the status of their claims, including any significant developments or changes. The frequency and detail of these reports can be tailored to the complexity of the claim and the client's preferences. For instance, in a straightforward claim, updates might be less frequent but still comprehensive, whereas a complex claim might necessitate more frequent, detailed updates. The key is to ensure that clients never feel out of the loop regarding their own cases.

Regular Updates

Consistency in updates is critical. Regular updates help in building a rhythm of communication that clients can rely on. These updates should not only inform clients about any new developments but also provide a brief overview of what has been done so far and what the next steps are. This approach helps in managing client expectations and reduces the anxiety associated with the uncertainty of the claims process. Even if there has been no significant progress, it's important to communicate this to the client, as it demonstrates attentiveness and commitment to their case.

Responsive Feedback Loop

Alongside providing updates, it's important to establish a

responsive feedback loop. This means being open to and addressing any questions or concerns the client may have in response to the updates. Encouraging clients to ask questions and providing clear, concise answers not only enhances their understanding but also reinforces their confidence in the adjuster's capabilities.

Providing timely updates and progress reports involves keeping clients informed about the status of their claims with regular, clear, and detailed communications. This practice is crucial in maintaining transparency, managing expectations, and building a trusting relationship. It ensures clients feel valued and reassured that their case is receiving the attention it deserves, thereby enhancing their overall experience with the public adjuster.

EXPLAINING COMPLEX INSURANCE CONCEPTS AND PHRASES

Simplifying Jargon

One of the most significant barriers in client communication within the insurance industry is the pervasive use of complex jargon and terminology. As Bill Wilson highlights in his book, "When Words Collide," even professionals within the insurance industry often grapple with the intricacies of insurance language. For clients, this complexity can be even more daunting. It is imperative for public adjusters to break down this terminology into language that is easily understandable by the layperson. This involves not just substituting complex terms with simpler words but also providing context and examples that make these concepts more relatable and easier to grasp.

When providing updates, clarity is key. Avoiding jargon and explaining terms or processes in layman's terms can greatly enhance client understanding and satisfaction. Additionally, providing a certain level of detail in these updates can be beneficial. This might include explaining the reasons behind delays, the outcomes of any negotiations with insurance companies, or the steps being taken to move the claim forward. This level of transparency and detail helps in building trust and reassures clients that their case is being handled with the utmost care and professionalism.

Process Demystification

The claims process, with its myriad steps and procedural nuances, can be overwhelming for clients. A key role of the public adjuster is to demystify this process, guiding clients through each stage with clarity and transparency. This involves explaining the purpose and importance of each step, what the client can expect, and how long it might take. By dissecting the process into manageable segments and walking the client through each one, the adjuster can alleviate much of the anxiety and confusion that clients may feel.

Additional Resources

Providing clients with supplementary materials or explanations can be extremely helpful in further clarifying complex concepts or processes. These resources could include written guides, diagrams, FAQs, or even video explanations that clients can refer to at their leisure. Such materials should be designed to be client-friendly, avoiding technical language and focusing on the key points most relevant to their situation.

Contextualizing Insurance Terms

In line with the insights from Wilson's "When Words Collide," it is beneficial to not only simplify terms but also to contextualize them within the framework of the client's specific claim. This means explaining how a particular term or concept directly impacts their claim. For example, when discussing terms like 'actual cash value' or 'replacement cost,' illustrate how these valuations would apply to their loss.

Interactive Explanations

Engaging clients in interactive explanations can also aid in their understanding. This could involve walking them through hypothetical scenarios, using visual aids, or even role-playing exercises to demonstrate how certain aspects of their claim will be handled. Interactive methods can be particularly effective in helping clients understand and retain complex information.

Feedback and Clarification

Regularly soliciting feedback from clients about their understanding of the process and terms can help identify areas that need further clarification. Encouraging clients to ask questions and providing clear, patient answers reinforce their understanding and comfort with the process.

HOW TO HANDLE CHALLENGING SITUATIONS AND MANAGE CLIENT EMOTIONS

Dealing with Dissatisfied or Frustrated Clients with Composure and Patience

In the face of dissatisfaction or frustration from clients, maintaining composure and patience is crucial. This involves keeping a calm demeanor, regardless of the intensity of the client's emotions. Demonstrating professionalism and understanding, even under pressure, helps in de-escalating tense situations. It's important to remember that the client's frustrations are often rooted in the stress of their situation rather than personal grievances against the adjuster.

Empathetic Listening

Active listening is a powerful tool in understanding and addressing client concerns. This involves not just hearing the words spoken but also paying attention to the emotions and underlying messages. Empathetic listening requires the adjuster to be fully present, acknowledging the client's feelings and validating their concerns. This approach helps clients feel heard and understood, which is often the first step in resolving their dissatisfaction.

Transparent Explanations

When setbacks occur, providing clear and transparent explanations is key. This involves openly discussing the reasons behind any delays or challenges and outlining the steps being taken to address them. Transparency helps in building trust and reassurance, showing clients that their concerns are being taken seriously and addressed proactively.

Tactical Empathy (from Chris Voss' "Never Split the Difference")

Voss emphasizes the use of tactical empathy, which involves understanding the feelings and mindset of another person and using that understanding to influence their behavior. In dealing with dissatisfied clients, it's important to recognize their emotions and demonstrate empathy towards their situation. This can be achieved by using reflective listening techniques, such as mirroring (repeating the last few words of what someone has just said) and labeling (naming the emotions the client might be feeling). These techniques help in building a connection and showing the client their feelings are acknowledged.

Calibrated Questions

Another strategy from Voss' book is the use of calibrated questions. These are open-ended questions that start with "how" or "what," which encourage the client to think and provide more information about their concerns. For example, asking "How can we make this right for you?" or "What is most important to you in resolving this issue?" These questions not only provide valuable insights into the client's priorities but also help them feel involved in finding a solution.

Reframing and Positive No

Voss also suggests the power of reframing a situation and using a "positive no." This involves presenting alternatives or solutions in a way that addresses the client's concerns while also setting realistic boundaries. For instance, if a client's expectation is unreasonable, rather than outright denial, the adjuster can offer alternative solutions that still aim to meet the client's core needs.

Handling dissatisfied or frustrated clients effectively involves a combination of composure, empathetic listening, transparent explanations, tactical empathy, calibrated questions, and the skillful use of reframing and positive responses. These strategies, inspired by Chris Voss' insights in "Never Split the Difference," can help public adjusters navigate challenging situations with clients, leading to more constructive outcomes and maintained relationships.

RESOLVING COMPLAINTS AND CONFLICT

Complaint Resolution Process

Establishing a structured process for handling and resolving client complaints is essential for maintaining professionalism and trust. This process should be clearly communicated to clients at the outset of their engagement with the public adjuster. It typically involves a step-by-step approach where complaints are first acknowledged, then investigated, and finally resolved. Each step should be handled with care and attention, ensuring the client feels their concerns are being taken seriously. The process should be designed to be as efficient as possible, minimizing the time between the complaint being raised and its resolution.

Proactive Solutions

When a complaint is raised, it is crucial to act swiftly and proactively. Quick action demonstrates to the client that their concerns are a priority. Solutions should be aimed at satisfying both parties, balancing the client's needs and the realities of the situation. This might involve offering alternative solutions, providing additional services, or sometimes, a simple acknowledgment and apology for any mistakes or misunderstandings. The key is to find a resolution that restores the client's confidence and trust in the adjuster's services.

Documentation

Keeping detailed records of all interactions and resolutions is crucial for future reference and accountability. This documentation should include the nature of the complaint, the steps taken to resolve it, and any communications with the client regarding the issue. In addition to serving as a record in case of future disputes, this documentation can also be a valuable tool for reviewing and improving the adjuster's practices and client service approach.

CONFIRMING WRITTEN FOLLOW-UP

Some situations may require confirming written follow-up in emails and letters that are professional, transparent, and empathetic. This written communication serves as an official record of the resolution process and ensures there is no ambiguity about what was discussed and agreed upon. The tone of these communications should be professional yet empathetic, acknowledging the client's concerns and clearly outlining the steps taken to address them. This not only provides a clear record but also reinforces the adjuster's commitment to resolving the client's concerns.

Compassionate Interactions

Demonstrating empathy and understanding in all communications is essential. This means actively listening to clients, validating their feelings, and responding in a way that shows genuine concern and compassion. Compassionate interactions involve more than just addressing the technical aspects of a claim; they require a human touch that acknowledges the client's emotional journey through the process.

Reassurance

Offering reassurance and support during challenging times is crucial in helping clients navigate the emotional aspects of their claim. This could involve affirming the client's feelings, providing positive feedback on the progress of their claim, or simply being present and available to discuss any concerns they may have. Reassurance can help alleviate some of the emotional burden clients may carry and can foster a sense of trust and safety in their relationship with the adjuster.

BALANCING EMPATHY WITH HONESTY

While it is important to act with empathy, the public adjuster must ensure this does not equate to giving false hope or agreeing to unrealistic expectations. Empathy must be balanced with honesty. This means being clear about what is realistically achievable and not agreeing to expected results that are unlikely to materialize. It also involves not affirming facts or documentation that does not exist or cannot be substantiated. Honesty in these situations, while potentially difficult, is crucial for maintaining integrity and trust in the long term.

Clear and Honest Communication

When communicating with empathy, it's important to be clear and honest about the realities of the claim process. This might involve discussing the potential challenges and limitations of the claim, the likelihood of various outcomes, and the timeframes involved. While these conversations can be difficult, they are necessary for setting realistic expectations and preventing future disappointments.

Empathy Without Misrepresentation

The public adjuster must navigate the fine line between being empathetic and inadvertently misrepresenting the situation. This involves being supportive and understanding, but also clear and forthright about the realities of the claim. It's about providing comfort and reassurance while also being truthful and transparent.

Managing client emotions with empathy involves a combination of emotional intelligence, compassionate interactions, reassurance, and a balance of empathy with honesty. Public adjusters must be adept at recognizing and responding to the emotional needs of their clients while also maintaining honesty and transparency about the realities of the claims process. This approach ensures that clients feel supported and understood, but also well-informed and prepared for the various outcomes of their claim.

RICH'S STORY

MANAGING CLIENT EXPECTATIONS

As Rich's public adjusting business grew, he quickly realized that managing client expectations was as crucial as handling the claims themselves. This lesson became particularly apparent when he found himself juggling the vastly different needs of residential and commercial clients.

The Anderson family, whose home was severely damaged by a fire, required a more personal touch. Rich learned that for residential clients like the Andersons, the emotional impact of losing their home was often as significant as the financial loss. He adapted his approach, offering not just professional expertise but also emotional support. Rich made a point of explaining each step of the process in simple terms, providing regular updates, and being available to address their concerns, no matter how small.

In contrast, when handling the claim for Dr. Ellis, a respected eye doctor whose clinic was damaged, Rich encountered a different set of expectations. Dr. Ellis was primarily concerned about the business interruption and its impact on his patients. Rich adjusted his communication style, focusing on concrete timelines, detailed financial projections, and strategies to minimize downtime. He learned to speak the language of business, providing Dr. Ellis with data-driven updates and clear action plans.

Through these experiences, Rich developed a nuanced approach to client management. For residential claims, he emphasized empathy, patience, and clear, jargon-free communication. For commercial claims, he adopted a more strategic, results-oriented approach, always keeping the client's business goals in mind.

Rich's ability to tailor his approach to different client types not only improved client satisfaction but also enhanced his reputation in the community. He learned that managing expectations wasn't about promising quick results, but about providing clarity, support, and expertise tailored to each client's unique situation.

CHAPTER 12
WHEN CLAIMS DON'T GO AS PLANNED

> The greatest glory in living lies not in never falling,
> but in rising every time we fall.
>
> NELSON MANDELA

AS A PUBLIC INSURANCE ADJUSTER, you should maintain these goals:

GOAL 1: Get your clients promptly paid.

GOAL 2: Get your clients fully paid.

If the carrier insists on choosing actions and decisions which prevent these goals, the public adjuster must consider another perspective:

GOAL 3: What are the best claim preparation steps to help the policyholder client to obtain full and prompt recovery and determine if the policyholder has other valuable rights as a result of the insurer's action and decisions?

Following a loss, getting the full amount of indemnity owed under the contract from the insurance company treasury and into the hands of the policyholder as fast as possible should be the goal of everybody in the claims industry. Every claim process resulting in action should be done in such a way as to accomplish this goal. Litigation, arbitration, meditation, and whatever other "-ation" we conjure in our resolution-oriented minds should only come about after the public adjuster fails in the best practices to reach the goal: *Get the policyholders fully and promptly paid.*

Policyholders do not come to public adjusters just to have their files sent to appraisal or litigation. These require additional costs and additional time to the detriment of the policyholder. Public adjusters should be wary of the ethical conflicts of interest if approached by appraisers or attorneys who seem to suggest that files are to be prepared for appraisal or litigation. This advice is usually a runaround to having the file sent to those suggesting this method of claims adjustment rather than focusing on actions and methods which are within the control of the public adjuster.

Public adjusters new to this field should not be taught that they are building a file for litigation. When people tell you that, you are being told an excuse for not resolving the claim. It is an easy excuse to turn over matters which may potentially cost your client money for all kinds of imperfections in your work and inability to master your craft. It is, however, a good idea to *document* every claim as if it were going to be shown to a judge and jury.

At the same time, it's important to get good legal advice on property insurance law and claims that are practical and lead to a policyholder's best resolution of a loss. Public adjusters should never practice law because it is illegal to do so, and there are times when legal advice is imperative. Public adjusters should seek legal help and practical advice from attorneys who are fully knowledgeable in property insurance law.

ASSESS THE VALIDITY OF THE CLAIM

Examine the Facts, Evidence, and Policy Coverage

Before suggesting the policyholder seek counsel, the best claims practice is for the public adjuster to reexamine the file. This step involves a meticulous review of all claim details, evidence collected, and the nuances of policy coverage. This process is crucial for establishing a request for the insurer to reexamine its decisions and actions. For example, in a windstorm claim involving water damage, it's essential to verify the cause of the water damage is covered under an insured peril and not limited. The public adjuster should be able to meet objections to coverage in an oral and written manner that is clear, based on facts which can be proven, and within the policy language. This step may involve analyzing incident reports, photographs of the damage, any relevant witness statements, expert reports, and the written explanation for the insurer's decisions. The goal is to establish a clear and factual basis for the claim, ensuring it falls within the scope of the policy's coverage.

Consult Experts

Engaging with experts is a critical aspect of assessing a claim's validity. In cases where specialized knowledge is required, such as the amount of damage from smoke, soot, and ash, consulting with forensic analysts can provide crucial insights to the cause, extent, and costs of remediation. These experts can offer an independent evaluation of the evidence, potentially uncovering details that might not be immediately apparent. Their expertise can be invaluable in complex scenarios, offering a level of detail and understanding that goes beyond the scope of a typical claim review. This step not only strengthens the claim's foundation but also prepares the public adjuster for any challenges that might arise if the only method for recovery is through the litigation process.

Investigative Techniques

Thorough investigative techniques of coverage and then of claim evaluation is essential for a comprehensive assessment of the claim. This includes interviewing witnesses to gather firsthand accounts of the incident, which can provide valuable insights into the events leading up to and following the damage. Visual evidence is vitally important. Additionally, reviewing surveillance footage can be instrumental in either corroborating the claimant's account of the event or uncovering potential discrepancies. In cases where fraud is suspected by the insurer, these investigative methods can be particularly crucial. They help in identifying any inconsistencies or anomalies which must be addressed. Mistakes or presumptions regarding facts by the insurer's adjuster must be raised by the public adjuster before the file is needlessly sent to counsel for the policyholder which would unnecessarily add costs and time to the policyholder's recovery.

ASSESS THE FINANCIAL IMPLICATIONS AND CONSIDER ALTERNATIVES TO LITIGATION

One ethical and legal obligation for all public adjusters is to not practice law. Many public adjusters unknowingly practice law by providing advice about the implications for going to litigation versus alternatives such as appraisal. When seeking advice from legal professionals as to which course of action to pursue, consider the facts of the case in relation to legal rights and principles. Advising a policyholder client to seek redress through appraisal is the practice of law rather than public adjusting. If the matter does not turn out well for the policyholder, it would be well within the policyholder's right to claim that the public adjuster committed malpractice and an ethical violation.

Good lawyers calculate the costs involved in pursuing the claim through litigation, including expert fees and potential litigation costs. They should analyze the claim's potential settlement value against the financial risks of litigation and appraisal. For example, a high-value property damage claim might warrant more resources in litigation due to a potentially larger settlement. Sometimes, the costs of experts are needed to be paid for by legal counsel willing to advance such costs after retention. The bottom line is that legal professionals experienced in the field should understand the legal implications and give informed advice to the policyholder about possible alternatives if the public adjuster is not able to obtain a favorable resolution.

Develop a Strategic Approach

A public adjuster should ask potential legal counsel whether a strategy should be developed considering the unique aspects of the claim, like prioritizing negotiation over litigation in a straightforward water damage claim where the insurer is simply not responding. In such a situation, identifying key issues and then objectives, such as achieving a fair settlement in a timely manner, can help develop a plan which serves the policyholder. Sometimes, a letter from counsel or a lawsuit sent along with a settlement demand may speed the process along. The paramount aspect is that each claim and each policyholder have unique facts which usually demand a somewhat different strategy.

Good attorneys anticipate insurers may challenge the public adjuster's assessment of the loss and reasons for extending coverage. Those attorneys should also be certain that all conditions precedent to filing a suit have been met and that all deadlines for filing suit still exist. The public adjuster is a key team player and must help assist providing these facts and claims-handling actions to legal counsel. The job of the public adjuster is to not simply turn over a file to the attorney but remain as a trusted advisor to the policyholder and aid the attorney.

CHOOSE A LAW FIRM TO WORK WITH

When settlement negotiations fail, a public adjuster has a crucial role in guiding policyholders through the next steps, particularly in suggesting possible lawyers to help obtain recovery. This role is multifaceted and involves understanding the policyholder's needs, knowledge of the legal landscape, and the ability to identify attorneys who constantly work for policyholders doing property insurance recovery, have resources to handle the matter, and a track record of success. The public adjuster must always remember that the policyholder has the absolute right to choose any attorney. The public adjuster must be careful to avoid any suggestion of a conflict of interest with the attorneys who may ultimately represent the policyholder and certainly not act as a capper or runner, which is unethical and usually criminal.

Understand the Policyholder's Needs

The first obligation of a public adjuster is to thoroughly understand the policyholder's situation and needs. This involves a comprehensive analysis of the claim, the reasons for the failure of settlement negotiations, and the specific challenges faced by the policyholder. For instance, if a claim has been denied due to alleged misrepresentation, the adjuster must recognize the need for an attorney with expertise in handling such disputes. Understanding the policyholder's financial constraints, desired timeline, and emotional state is also crucial. This empathetic approach ensures the adjuster can provide tailored advice that aligns with the policyholder's unique circumstances.

Know the Legal Landscape

A public adjuster must possess a broad understanding of the legal landscape related to insurance claims. This includes knowledge of various law firms' reputations, areas of specialization, and track records. An adjuster should be aware of the latest legal trends, significant court rulings, and changes in insurance law that could impact the policyholder's case. This knowledge enables the adjuster to make informed recommendations about which legal firms or attorneys are best suited to handle the specific nuances of the claim.

Identify Attorneys who Concentrate a Legal Practice in the Representation of Policyholders

The public adjuster must be adept at identifying attorneys who specialize or limit their practice to insurance recovery filed and have a proven track record of success in similar cases. This involves researching and compiling a list of potential lawyers or law firms that have successfully handled claims similar to the policyholder's. The public adjuster should consider factors such as the attorney's experience in dealing with the particular insurance company involved, their success rate in similar cases, and their approach to client communication and case management. The policyholder should be advised that choosing attorneys through advertising is not the best method for selection of legal counsel. Reputation, experience, credentials, and success should be core considerations for those whom the policyholder should first seek assistance. Advertising leads to puffery of qualifications, even in the legal field.

Facilitate Initial Contact

Once potential attorneys have been identified, the public adjuster may facilitate the initial contact between the policyholder and the legal firm. This might involve setting up consultations, providing the attorney with preliminary claim details, and assisting the policyholder in preparing for these meetings. The adjuster's role here is to ensure the policyholder feels supported and informed throughout this transition. Many attorneys demand the policyholder call or contact the attorney directly to avoid any accusations of case running or improper conduct. Attorneys who provide their contracts to public adjusters directly, through a website, or indirectly asking the public adjuster to have the policyholder client sign the attorney's contract should be avoided and possibly reported to the Bar. The potential attorney should speak with, review the file, and personally enter into the retention contract. The public adjuster should never be part of an attorney's retention process.

Provide a Balanced Perspective

It is essential for the public adjuster to demand from the potential lawyer a balanced perspective on the potential outcomes of pursuing legal action, which should be explained by legal counsel. This includes discussing the possible timeframes, costs involved, and the likelihood of success. The public adjuster should also ask the legal counsel to prepare the policyholder for the realities of legal proceedings, including the potential for lengthy processes and the emotional toll it can take. The public adjuster should reassure the policyholder that they are there through every step of the process.

SUGGESTIONS BY THE PUBLIC ADJUSTER FOR THE POLICYHOLDER TO ASK POTENTIAL LAWYERS

When a public adjuster is guiding a policyholder in selecting a lawyer, especially in the context of failed settlement negotiations, it's crucial to suggest a set of targeted questions that align with the key areas of researching and evaluating potential legal firms, as well as assessing compatibility and alignment. These questions should help the policyholder make an informed decision about which attorney or law firm is best suited to their specific needs and circumstances.

Track Record and Expertise

- "Can you describe your experience in handling cases similar to mine?"
- "What is your success rate in insurance claim disputes or litigation?"

- "Can you provide examples of past cases you've handled that are similar to my situation?"

Reputation and Recommendations

- "How did you acquire your expertise in insurance law?"
- "Are there any client testimonials or references I can review?"
- "Have you received any professional recognition or awards in your field?"
- "Has a Judge ever appointed you in a leadership role or noted your expertise?"
- "Have you or others in your firm been subject to disciplinary actions?"

Resources and Capacity

- "Does your firm have the financial and people resources to handle my case effectively?"
- "How do you manage cases with complex or extensive documentation?"
- "Are there other professionals in your firm who will work on my case, and what are their qualifications?"

Firm's Values and Culture

- "What are the core values of your law firm?"
- "How do those values influence your approach to handling cases?"
- "Can you describe the culture within your firm and how it impacts client relationships?"

Communication Style and Collaboration

- "How do you typically communicate with clients during a case?"
- "What is your approach to client involvement and decision-making in the legal process?"
- "How do you handle disagreements or differing opinions with clients?"

Approach and Legal Strategies

- "Can you outline your general strategy for a case like mine?"
- "How do you adapt your strategy in response to unexpected developments in a case?"
- "What is your approach to negotiation versus litigation in insurance disputes?"

Client Support and Engagement

- "How do you ensure that clients are kept informed and involved throughout the case?"
- "What support do you provide to clients to help them understand the legal process and their options?"
- "How do you handle client concerns or questions during the course of a case?"

ONGOING SUPPORT AND COMMUNICATION

Even after referring a policyholder to a lawyer, the adjuster's role does not end. They should remain available to provide ongoing support, answer any further questions, and assist in communication between the policyholder and the attorney. This ongoing support ensures the policyholder feels continuously guided and supported throughout the legal process.

Create a Working Relationship with a First-Party Law Firm

Creating a productive and effective working relationship with a first-party law firm is a critical component of successfully navigating the complexities of insurance claims and seeking help in the business of public adjusting. This relationship is built on effective communication, comprehensive information sharing, and collaborative strategy development where the attorney can help provide legal analysis and practical guidance to a public adjuster when no litigation may occur. An attorney who is caring and knowledgeable about the business of public adjusting can be seen as a trusted advisor.

Establish Effective Communication Channels

If a client of a public adjuster selects the attorney, the public adjuster should inquire about establishing structured communication channels which are essential for regular updates and consistent information flow to the policyholder client. Good law firms and lawyers insist on this and are happy to find a public adjuster taking ongoing interest for the benefit of a common client. This could involve scheduling weekly calls or meetings to discuss the progress of the claim, any new developments, and the next steps. Regular communication helps in maintaining momentum and ensures both parties are aligned in their approach. There are always times when such meetings must be without the public adjuster attending to be certain of maintaining attorney-client privilege. The point is that the public adjuster is certain the client is being taken care of, and the case is moving along diligently.

Preferred Modes

It's important to agree on preferred communication methods that suit both parties. Some may prefer the immediacy of phone calls, while others might opt for the documentation trail of emails. In some cases, in-person meetings might be necessary for more detailed discussions. The key is to find a balance that ensures efficient and effective communication.

Open Dialogue

Maintaining an open and transparent dialogue throughout the process is crucial. This involves being honest about challenges, setbacks, and uncertainties. An environment where both parties can freely express concerns and ideas fosters trust and leads to more effective problem-solving.

SHARE ESSENTIAL CLAIM INFORMATION

Documentation

Providing the entire and comprehensive claim file documentation is fundamental. This includes everything — even duplicates of photographs of the damage, repair estimates, incident reports, and all correspondence related to the claim. Detailed documentation forms the backbone of the case and assists the legal team in understanding the full scope of the claim. This also includes all emails between the client and the public adjuster. The public adjuster should anticipate that the insurance company will subpoena all file materials later in litigation. So, it should first be completely turned over to the policyholder's attorney for thorough review prior to filing a lawsuit. Good attorneys analyze the file before the suit is filed.

Policy Details

Sharing all relevant policy information, including any prior claim history, is crucial. This helps the legal team in understanding the coverage nuances and any precedents that might influence the current claim.

Case Building

Most claim files should build a robust case for coverage based on simply reading the file. The insights of the public adjuster and arguments advocating for coverage in a professional and likable manner should be obviously present. All angles of the claim should be covered, and the strongest possible case should be presented by the public adjuster before counsel is retained. It's about creating a narrative that accurately represents the policyholder's situation and substantiates coverage and the amount of the claim.

COLLABORATE AND COOPERATE

Strategy Development

Good attorneys should enjoy having a professional public adjuster on the team. They should ask about developing a unified strategy which the public adjuster may have from particular knowledge of the defendant or the case. Good law firms familiar with working with public adjusters ask many questions and sometimes ask for guidance, knowing teams are stronger than individuals. Great attorneys lack arrogance and have strong-enough egos and emotional intelligence to know public adjusters can help them win their common client's case. Both parties should work together to determine the best course of action based on the specifics of the case for the common good of the client with the attorney having the ultimate say in legal strategy.

Share Information

Timely and efficient sharing of information and necessary documentation is vital. This ensures the legal team has all the resources they need to effectively represent the policyholder. Fostering a cooperative and positive relationship benefits the policyholder. Mutual respect and understanding facilitate smoother collaboration and a more effective partnership which should result in faster recoveries for the policyholder.

MANAGE EXPECTATIONS AND TIMELINES

Realistic Expectations

It's important to set and manage realistic expectations regarding the outcomes and timelines of the claim. This involves understanding the complexities of legal proceedings and the time they might take, as well as the unpredictability of negotiation processes. A public adjuster should not be afraid to ask about these time frames because the policyholder may ask for assurances as well.

Keeping all parties informed about the claim's progress in litigation is an essential job of the attorney. Regular updates from attorneys help in managing expectations and keeping the policyholder reassured. The public adjuster can be proactive in addressing delays or challenges that arise and by providing additional insights which the policyholder's selected law firm and its attorneys may not be aware of. This might involve asking questions and making suggestions in response to developments in the case or overcoming obstacles that arise during the litigation process. Good attorneys do not expect the policyholder's public adjuster to be a wallflower not actively participating but seeking to help. A great legal team involves a hardworking, ethical, and passionate public adjuster.

RICH'S STORY

WHEN CLAIMS DON'T GO AS PLANNED

Rich's journey in public adjusting had taught him many lessons, but one of the most crucial was learning to navigate claims that didn't go as planned. He encountered numerous obstacles, from insurance companies disputing damage assessments to unforeseen complications in the restoration process. These challenges tested Rich's problem-solving skills and reinforced the importance of adaptability in his profession.

One particularly complex case involved Mr. Thompson, whose family-owned manufacturing business had been devastated by a recent fire. As Rich delved into the claim, he encountered intricate policy interpretations and potential coverage disputes that pushed the boundaries of his expertise. Recognizing the need for specialized legal insight, Rich made the decision to consult with Skip Berlin, a renowned attorney in property insurance law.

Rich's choice to bring in Skip demonstrated his commitment to serving his clients' best interests, even if it meant acknowledging the limits of his own knowledge. Skip's expertise proved invaluable as he navigated the legal intricacies of Mr. Thompson's policy, uncovering clauses and precedents that strengthened their position.

Working alongside Skip, Rich gained a deeper understanding of the legal aspects of claims handling. This collaboration not only helped resolve Mr. Thompson's case more favorably but also enhanced Rich's ability to handle complex claims in the future. He learned the importance of recognizing when to seek expert assistance and how to integrate legal strategies into his claims handling process.

The experience with Mr. Thompson's case and working with Skip Berlin marked a turning point in Rich's career. It broadened his perspective on claim resolution and reinforced the value of building a network of specialists to support his work. Rich emerged from this experience with renewed confidence in his ability to tackle even the most challenging claims, knowing when and how to leverage external expertise for his clients' benefit.

PART FIVE

ADVANCED BUSINESS GROWTH

CHAPTER 13
PROFESSIONAL DEVELOPMENT

THE EVER-EVOLVING INSURANCE INDUSTRY

> An investment in knowledge pays the best interest.
>
> BENJAMIN FRANKLIN

THE INSURANCE INDUSTRY is characterized by its dynamic and ever-evolving nature. This constant state of flux necessitates a commitment to continuous learning for public insurance adjusters. As insurance policy forms, insurance laws and regulations, and market conditions change, public adjusters must stay informed and adapt. This ongoing education is not just a requirement but a strategic tool for staying effective and running a successful public adjusting business.

TECHNOLOGICAL, REGULATORY, AND MARKET CHANGES

The impact of technological advancements cannot be overstated. From AI-driven claims processing to digital communication channels to drone usage, technology is reshaping how insurance claims are handled. Additionally, laws and regulations change constantly and require public adjusters to be perpetually updated regarding codes and case law which ensure compliance and proper handling of claims. Market trends, such as the increasing frequency of natural disasters due to climate change, also significantly impact the industry, dictating a need for public adjusters to consider where they conduct their business, they need to emphasize greater expertise. For example, if your location is just north of Dallas, you should have an extraordinary amount of knowledge about hailstorm losses, with increased emphasis of ongoing study regarding nuances of policy language, investigative steps, pricing, and law regarding these types of losses.

ADAPT TO REMAIN COMPETITIVE

In this rapidly changing environment, adaptability is key. Public insurance adjusters must embrace new developments to maintain a competitive edge. This includes understanding new insurance policies, adapting to technological tools, and being aware of changing customer expectations. *The Lean Startup* by Eric Ries delves into the importance of building a sustainable business model that can withstand the challenges of a rapidly changing market and technological landscape. Ries emphasizes the need for continuous innovation and responsiveness, especially to the treatment of customers and clients, arguing that these are crucial for long-term success in an increasingly competitive and unpredictable business environment.

ADVANTAGES OF NICHE EXPERTISE

Everybody should be concerned about being a "jack of all trades and a master of none." Would you rather have a general surgeon or a neurosurgeon if you were faced with brain surgery? Specializing in niche markets, whether defined by business type, property type, or claim type, offers significant advantages. It allows public adjusters to become deeply knowledgeable in specific areas, setting them apart as experts. This expertise not only benefits their clients but also enhances their professional reputation.

It certainly can change the selling proposition of a public adjuster when marketing services to a particular client. Specializing in niche claims provides public adjusters with substantial marketing advantages. By focusing on specific areas, such as a particular type of client with a particular type of property loss or claim, public adjusters can develop deep expertise akin to a neurosurgeon's specialized skills compared to a general surgeon. This specialization positions them as experts in their field, significantly enhancing their appeal to potential clients who seek specialized knowledge for their unique needs. Such expertise not only elevates the adjuster's professional reputation but also fosters trust and credibility among clients. In a market crowded with generalists, niche specialists stand out, attracting clients who value and are willing to invest in top-tier, specialized services. This targeted expertise allows for more effective marketing strategies, as adjusters can tailor their messaging to resonate with specific client groups, leading to higher client acquisition and retention rates. In essence, niche specialization transforms public adjusters into sought-after experts, offering a clear competitive edge in the marketing landscape.

CAREER ADVANCEMENT AND CREDIBILITY

Specialization can lead to career advancement and increased credibility. This specialization also often results in a deeper understanding of the unique challenges and solutions within that claim niche. By focusing on a particular niche, public adjusters can build a strong reputation leading to more referrals and being sought after as an expert able to resolve the particular problem faced by the policyholder.

EDUCATION AND CONFIDENCE

Benjamin Franklin has been quoted as saying that "an investment in knowledge pays the best interest." The journey of ongoing education and professional growth is pivotal in building a public adjuster's confidence. This process involves more than just acquiring knowledge; it's about developing a deep understanding and expertise in the field. Such expertise enables adjusters to make well-informed decisions, communicate with clarity and conviction, and handle complex claims with a level of assurance that only comes from a solid educational foundation. This confidence is not just internal; it radiates outward, influencing how public adjusters are perceived by clients, colleagues, and adjusters for the insurance company. It empowers them to approach challenging situations with a mindset which provides solutions that are innovative, practical, and accepted.

PROFESSIONALISM AND TRUST

Former Harvard Business School professor David Maister in *True Professionalism: The Courage to Care about Your People, Your Clients, and Your Career* argues true professionalism goes beyond technical expertise and includes a deep, genuine commitment to the interests of clients, colleagues, and one's own career. He emphasizes professionals must care deeply about their work and the people they serve, advocating for a client-first approach in all business dealings. This involves not just meeting but exceeding client expectations, fostering trust, and building long-term relationships.

Continuous learning is a key component in enhancing an

adjuster's professionalism. It reflects a dedication to their craft and a commitment to staying abreast of the latest trends, technologies, and regulatory changes in the insurance industry. This commitment fosters trust among clients and peers, as they recognize the adjuster's effort to remain current and competent in their field. A well-informed adjuster, who is up to date with industry developments, is more likely to earn respect and trust, which are essential in building long-lasting professional relationships.

MAINTAINING HIGH STANDARDS

Standards of practice are a key aspect of professionalism. It's not just about being knowledgeable; it's also about being ethical and effective in applying that knowledge (more about ethics in Chapter 14). Continuous education ensures adjusters are not only aware of the best practices and legal requirements of their profession but are also skilled in implementing them. This commitment to excellence in practice not only benefits the adjusters in their professional growth but also upholds the integrity of the field, ensuring clients receive the highest quality of service. In essence, the pursuit of professional development is a commitment to excellence, a hallmark of true professionalism in the dynamic and demanding world of public insurance adjusting.

MONITORING INDUSTRY TRENDS

Importance of Being Informed

In the dynamic field of public insurance adjusting, staying informed about emerging trends is not just beneficial; it's essential. This vigilance enables adjusters to anticipate and adapt to changes in the industry, ensuring they remain relevant and effective. By understanding new developments, whether they're technological advancements, shifts in policyholder needs, or changes in regulatory landscapes, adjusters can refine their strategies and methodologies. This proactive approach is crucial in providing the best possible service to clients, as it allows adjusters to offer informed advice and innovative solutions that align with the latest industry standards.

Sources for Industry News

To stay abreast of these changes, adjusters should regularly engage with a variety of information sources. This includes subscribing to industry journals and newsletters, visiting websites dedicated to insurance news, and participating in online forums and professional networks. These resources provide a wealth of information, from in-depth analyses of market trends to updates on legal and regulatory changes affecting the industry. Additionally, public adjusters should leverage social media platforms and professional groups where other public adjusters engage, as they often serve as hubs for real-time discussions and insights from industry peers and thought leaders.

Benefits of Industry Events

Beyond digital and print media, attending conferences, webinars, and industry events is invaluable for staying informed and connected. These events are not just about absorbing information; they offer a platform for interactive learning and networking. Conferences and seminars often feature expert speakers discussing current trends and forecasting future directions of the industry. Workshops and panel discussions provide opportunities for adjusters to engage with these topics actively, while networking sessions open doors to collaborations and partnerships. These events also serve as a barometer for the industry's pulse, offering a glimpse into the collective challenges and opportunities being faced by professionals in the field.

Engaging With Professional Public Adjuster Associations

In addition to these resources, involvement with professional adjusting organizations and public adjuster associations is highly beneficial. These organizations often conduct research, publish presentations of specific areas of claim handling, and offer training sessions specifically tailored to the needs of public adjusters. They also play a pivotal role in advocating for the profession, influencing policy, and setting industry standards. Active participation in these bodies not only keeps adjusters informed but also contributes to their professional development and standing within the community.

INDUSTRY ASSOCIATIONS AND NETWORKING

Role of Industry Associations

Industry associations are pivotal in shaping the landscape of public insurance adjusting. They serve as a nexus for professional development, offering a wealth of resources, training programs, and opportunities for collaboration. These associations often spearhead initiatives to standardize practices, advocate for the profession, and influence policymaking. By providing up-to-date information, guidelines, and best practices, they help adjusters stay informed and compliant with industry standards. Furthermore, these bodies often facilitate certification programs and continuing education courses, which are crucial for public adjusters looking to advance their skills and credentials.

Networking Opportunities

The value of networking in this field cannot be overstated. Engaging with industry peers and experts opens doors to a world of shared experiences, diverse perspectives, and collective wisdom. Networking events, whether they are conferences, seminars, or informal meetups, offer a platform for adjusters to connect with others who share similar challenges and goals. These interactions can lead to fruitful collaborations, mentorship opportunities, and even business partnerships. Networking also keeps adjusters in tune with the pulse of the industry, providing insights into emerging trends, new technologies, and evolving client expectations.

Sharing Knowledge and Insights

A network of professionals serves as a rich repository of knowledge and insights. Through interactions within these networks, public adjusters can learn from the successes and failures of their peers, gaining a broader understanding of the industry. This collaborative environment fosters a culture of knowledge sharing, where ideas and strategies are exchanged, and innovative solutions are born. Such exchanges can be particularly beneficial in navigating complex claims, understanding new regulatory changes, or implementing cutting-edge technologies and techniques in the claims process.

Building a Professional Identity

Networking and active participation in industry associations also play a crucial role in building a professional and reputation identity. They provide adjusters with a platform to establish themselves as thought leaders and experts in their field. Contributing to discussions, presenting at events, or writing articles for industry publications are ways public adjusters can enhance their professional reputation and visibility.

Leveraging Digital Platforms

In today's digital age, online platforms have become an integral part of networking and professional development. Social media, online forums, and virtual conferences offer additional avenues for adjusters to connect with their peers globally. These digital platforms are often supported by associations, providing accessibility for public adjusters to engage with industry conversations, share insights, and stay updated on developments, regardless of their geographical location.

Cultivating a Supportive Community

Beyond professional growth, these associations and networks cultivate a supportive community. They provide a sense of belonging and a shared purpose, which is essential in a field that can often be challenging and competitive. This sense of community is vital for personal well-being and professional resilience, enabling adjusters to thrive in their careers.

MENTORSHIP AND COACHING

Advantages of Mentorship

Mentorship and coaching stand as cornerstones in the professional development of public insurance adjusters. These relationships offer a unique blend of personalized guidance, support, and experiential learning. For adjusters, having a mentor means having access to a trusted advisor who can provide insights based on real-world experiences. This relationship is invaluable in helping new adjusters navigate the complexities of the industry, offering a safe space to discuss challenges, brainstorm solutions, and receive constructive feedback. Mentors can also help in setting realistic career goals and devising strategies to achieve them, thereby accelerating professional growth.

Mentorship Programs

Recognizing the value of mentorship, many organizations and associations within the public insurance adjusting industry have established formal mentorship programs. These programs are designed to pair less-experienced adjusters with veterans in the field. The objective is to facilitate a structured transfer of knowledge and skills, ensuring the next generation of adjusters is well-equipped to uphold the standards of the profession. These programs often include regular meetings, goal setting, and progress reviews, providing a comprehensive framework for professional development.

Learning From Experienced Professionals

Engaging with experienced professionals through mentorship can significantly enhance an adjuster's learning curve. Mentors provide a wealth of knowledge gained from years of practice, offering insights into the nuances of claim handling, client relations, and ethical dilemmas. This practical perspective is crucial for understanding how to apply theoretical knowledge in real-world scenarios. Mentors can share stories of their successes and failures, offering lessons that are often not found in textbooks or classrooms.

Benefits of Coaching

While mentorship focuses on sharing experience and guidance, coaching is another vital tool that focuses on developing specific skills and competencies. Coaches work with public adjusters to identify areas for improvement, set achievable goals, and develop strategies to reach these goals. This process often involves a more structured approach, including regular sessions, exercises, and feedback mechanisms.

Networking and Career Opportunities

Mentorship and coaching also open doors to networking and career opportunities. Mentors often introduce mentees to their professional networks, which can lead to new connections, collaborations, and even job opportunities. This exposure is invaluable for public adjusters looking to establish themselves in the industry.

Personalized Development Plan

A key advantage of mentorship and coaching is the creation of a personalized development plan. This plan is tailored to the individual's strengths, weaknesses, and career aspirations. It provides a road map for professional growth, ensuring the public adjuster remains focused and motivated. The goal is to visualize what the ideal public adjuster would be and then develop a plan to achieve that goal. Mentorship helps keep the public adjuster on track by having somebody to report to for accountability and motivation.

Emotional Support and Encouragement

Beyond skill development and career guidance, mentors and coaches often provide emotional support. They can act as sounding boards during challenging times, offering encouragement, and helping adjusters maintain a positive outlook. The work of public adjusting is arduous and detailed. Having an empathetic person who is meeting with a public adjuster on a regular basis is motivating and a good investment for one to make for themselves.

SELF-DIRECTED LEARNING AND PERSONAL DEVELOPMENT

In the ever-evolving field of public insurance adjusting, self-directed learning is a vital component of professional growth. This approach allows adjusters to take charge of their educational journey, selecting resources and topics that align with their specific needs and interests. By engaging in self-directed learning, adjusters can delve into areas that are directly relevant to their work or explore new subjects that may offer future benefits. This can include reading industry-specific books, conducting research on emerging trends, or utilizing online courses and webinars. The flexibility and autonomy of self-directed learning make it an effective way for adjusters to stay current and deepen their expertise.

Personal Development Strategies

Beyond technical knowledge, personal development strategies play a crucial role in an adjuster's professional journey. Developing skills such as leadership, effective communication, and strategic decision-making is crucial. These skills enhance an adjuster's ability to lead teams, manage client relationships, and navigate complex situations. For instance, strong communication skills are essential for clearly explaining policy details to clients or negotiating with insurance companies. Similarly, effective leadership and decision-making skills are vital for guiding teams through challenging claims processes. Investing time in developing these soft skills can significantly impact an adjuster's professional effectiveness and career trajectory. Because negotiation and listening are so important, Chris Voss' book, *Never Split The Difference* and his workshops are items in the "must learn from" category for all public adjusters.

Value of Continuous Self-Improvement

In a dynamic industry like public insurance adjusting, continuous self-improvement is not just beneficial; it's a necessity. The field is characterized by frequent regulatory changes, evolving market conditions, and advancements in technology. Adjusters who commit to ongoing learning and self-improvement ensure they remain competent and confident in their roles. This commitment to excellence is reflected in the quality of service they provide to clients, enhancing their reputation and success in the industry. Continuous self-improvement also fosters a mindset of adaptability and resilience, enabling adjusters to effectively respond to new challenges and opportunities.

Expanding Knowledge Horizons

Self-directed learning also involves expanding one's knowledge horizons beyond the immediate scope of public insurance adjusting. This could include understanding related fields, such as law, construction, or property valuation. Such interdisciplinary knowledge can provide adjusters with a more holistic understanding of the claims process and enable them to offer more comprehensive services to their clients. The important aspect is to keep this learning relevant to other areas of public adjusting practice. The question should be— "how is learning this subject going to make me a better public adjuster?"

LEVERAGING TECHNOLOGY FOR LEARNING

In today's digital age, public adjusters have access to a plethora of online resources and tools that can facilitate self-directed learning. For example, subscribing to and reading *Property Insurance Coverage Law Blog* daily will result in keeping up with many changes in property insurance law. The blog has a search feature which allows public adjusters to research any number of specific articles about claims-handling issues and the law. Other online platforms, educational websites, and virtual communities offer convenient and accessible ways to acquire new knowledge and skills. Adjusters can leverage these technologies to engage in interactive learning experiences, participate in online forums, and stay connected with global industry trends.

Setting Personal Goals and Milestones

For anybody setting a personal goal and attempting to reach it through self-study, I would suggest watching the YouTube video by Dr. Justin Sung, *"How I changed my life in 334 days with Reverse Goal Setting."* Sung outlines crucial steps as being the identification of the goal, your current status, and imagining the person who can achieve this goal. He suggests that by creating realistic deadlines, people can make significant changes. An important aspect of self-directed learning and personal development is setting clear personal goals and milestones. This helps adjusters maintain focus and measure their progress. Whether it's mastering a new claim processing software, becoming fluent in industry regulations, or developing leadership skills, setting specific objectives with milestones is the key to direction and motivation.

RICH'S STORY

PROFESSIONAL DEVELOPMENT

Rich's commitment to excellence in public adjusting led him to recognize the value of continuous professional development. As his company grew and handled an increasing variety of claims, Rich realized that to truly excel, he needed to focus his expertise and seek specialized knowledge. This insight prompted him to hire Annette Elder, a renowned professional coach specializing in public adjusting companies.

Working with Annette opened Rich's eyes to new possibilities in his field. Through their sessions, Rich gained clarity on his strengths and the areas where he could make the most significant impact. Annette helped him identify patterns in the types of claims he found most engaging and where his team seemed to excel.

As they analyzed his company's performance and market trends, Rich decided to specialize in water damage claims, particularly those resulting from severe weather events. This decision was influenced by the increasing frequency of such incidents in his region and his team's proven track record in handling these complex cases.

With his new focus, Rich embarked on an intensive

educational journey. He enrolled in advanced courses on water damage restoration, mold remediation, and structural drying techniques. Recognizing the importance of professional credentials, Rich also pursued the Senior Professional Public Adjuster (SPPA®) designation from The Institutes, a highly respected certification in the industry.

Annette guided Rich in creating a professional development plan for his entire team, ensuring that everyone's skills aligned with the company's new specialization. This focused approach not only improved their technical expertise but also boosted team morale and efficiency.

Rich's commitment to professional development and specialization paid off. His company became known as the go-to experts for water damage claims, attracting more complex and high-value cases. Rich found that by narrowing his focus, he had actually expanded his business's potential, proving that continuous learning and specialization were key to success in the ever-evolving field of public adjusting.

CHAPTER 14
ETHICAL PRACTICES

> Ethics is knowing the difference between what you have a right to do and what is right to do.
>
> POTTER STEWART

ETHICAL CONDUCT and customer-centric service are not just best practices; they are essential components that define the very essence of the public adjusting profession. This chapter delves into how ethical practices, intertwined with exceptional customer service contribute significantly to building lasting relationships, a reputable brand and promote the profession. The importance of adhering to industry regulations and ethical standards, the art of providing exceptional customer service, and the public adjuster's fiduciary responsibilities are aimed at fostering trust and professionalism.

UNDERSTAND ETHICAL RESPONSIBILITIES

Define Ethical Conduct

Ethical conduct in public insurance adjusting is a

multifaceted concept, intricately woven from the threads of integrity, honesty, and transparency. It is about making decisions that not only comply with legal standards but also uphold the highest moral principles. This conduct extends beyond mere adherence to the laws and regulations found in state codes and the department of insurance regulations. It involves a deep-rooted commitment to professional work which promotes fairness and justice. Ethical conduct is the guiding light that ensures every action and decision is made with a sense of responsibility and moral clarity, setting a standard of excellence in the profession.

Impact on Stakeholders

Ethical behavior has a profound and far-reaching impact on policyholders, insurance carriers, and the broader insurance industry. It shapes the foundation of trust, influences, perceptions and sets the tone for claims handling standards. Ethical conduct fosters a positive environment where policyholders feel valued and respected, insurance carriers operate in a fair and equitable manner, and the entire public adjusting profession is seen in a positive light. This ripple effect of ethical behavior reinforces the importance of maintaining high ethical standards in every aspect of public insurance adjusting.

Importance of Integrity

Integrity is the cornerstone of all business dealings in the field of public insurance adjusting. It is about consistently doing the right thing, even when no one is watching, ensuring every action and decision aligns with moral and ethical values. Integrity involves a steadfast adherence to a set of ethical principles, guiding public adjusters in their interactions with policyholders and representatives of the insurer. It is a commitment to honesty, fairness, and transparency in all dealings, which builds trust and credibility. This unwavering dedication to integrity is what distinguishes exceptional public adjusters who foster a culture of trust and respect within the insurance industry.

ADHERE TO INDUSTRY REGULATIONS AND STANDARDS

Familiarization with Regulations

Mastery of the regulations and guidelines governing the public insurance adjusting industry is not just a requirement but a fundamental responsibility. This encompasses a thorough understanding of the nuances and intricacies of state laws and regulations that directly impact all duties of public adjusters and insurance claim practices. An adjuster's proficiency in claims handling ensures that the public adjuster is well-equipped to navigate whatever complex legal nuances and issues may arise in any individual claims. This knowledge is not static; it requires continuous updating and understanding of evolving laws and regulations, ensuring public adjusters remain compliant, informed, and conduct work in a professional manner.

Compliance

Compliance with legal and ethical requirements transcends mere adherence to rules and regulations. Compliance is about understanding the spirit of the law, not just the letter, and applying this understanding in every aspect of the adjusting process. It involves a proactive approach to staying abreast of regulatory changes and integrating them into daily practices. This commitment to compliance safeguards the interests of policyholders and upholds the integrity of the adjusting process.

Uphold Standards

Professional standards act as the bedrock of policyholder protection. They are not just guidelines but essential principles that guide ethical decision-making and professional conduct. They are found in laws and the ethical standards of various public adjuster trade organizations. Upholding these standards is crucial for maintaining the dignity and respect of the profession. It involves a commitment to best practices, ethical dealings, and a dedication to the highest level of professionalism. These standards serve as a moral compass, guiding adjusters in their interactions with policyholders, ensuring their actions are always in the best interest of those they serve. Upholding these standards is a testament to a public adjuster's dedication to excellence and integrity in their profession.

An example of professional ethical standards is found in the American Association of Public Insurance Adjusters (AAPIA) Ethical Code.

AVOID CONFLICTS OF INTEREST

Identify Conflicts

Recognizing potential conflicts of interest is a critical proactive measure in upholding ethical standards within the public insurance adjusting sector. This process requires a high level of vigilance and a commitment to transparency, especially with the policyholder. Public adjusters must identify situations that could potentially compromise their objectivity or appear to do so. This involves a thorough assessment of each case, ensuring personal, financial, or other interests do not conflict with the adjuster's professional duties. If a conflict arises, transparency and best practice requires the issue be disclosed and resolved in writing.

Prioritize Policyholders

Placing the needs and best interests of policyholders at the forefront is the essence of a customer-centric approach in public insurance adjusting. This commitment goes beyond mere service delivery; it is about ensuring every decision and action taken is in the best interest of the policyholder. This approach requires a deep understanding of the policyholder's situation, needs and a dedication to acting as their advocate. Indeed, some states by law require the public adjuster to act in the highest representative capacity as a fiduciary to and for the policyholder. By prioritizing policyholders, adjusters demonstrate their commitment to fairness and ethical practice, thereby fostering trust and building long-lasting relationships.

Manage Conflicts

Establishing and adhering to clear procedures to address conflicts of interest is fundamental in maintaining ethical integrity. These procedures should be designed to ensure all decisions are made with impartiality and integrity. This involves setting up systems to disclose potential conflicts, seeking guidance from peers or supervisors when needed, and where necessary, recusing oneself from cases where impartiality cannot be guaranteed. Effective management of conflicts of interest is crucial in preserving the trust of policyholders and upholding the reputation of the adjusting profession. It is about making decisions that are not only fair and unbiased but are also perceived to be so by all involved parties.

THE PUBLIC ADJUSTER ACTING AS A FIDUCIARY

Fiduciaries hold a critical role in various contexts, such as legal, financial, and trust-related matters. Their typical duties, which are grounded in trust and ethical conduct, include:

Duty of Loyalty

This is perhaps the most fundamental duty of a fiduciary. It requires the fiduciary to act solely in the best interests of the policyholder client, above their own interests or the interests of third parties. This means avoiding conflicts of interest and not profiting from their position as a public adjuster at the expense of the policyholder.

Duty of Care

A fiduciary must exercise a high standard of care in managing the assets or affairs of the beneficiary. This involves making informed and prudent decisions, like how a reasonably cautious person would manage their own affairs. It includes conducting thorough research and due diligence before making decisions.

Duty to Act in Good Faith

Fiduciaries are required to act honestly and in good faith when dealing with policyholder clients. This means being transparent, providing accurate information, and not misleading or deceiving the policyholder in any way.

Duty to Provide Information

A fiduciary should keep the beneficiary informed about relevant information concerning their assets or interests. This includes regular updates and reports on the status of the adjustment, or any actions taken on their behalf. Public adjusters should not withhold information gained from their clients.

Duty of Confidentiality

Fiduciaries must maintain the confidentiality of information related to the policyholder or their claims. They should not disclose any sensitive information without proper authorization or legal requirement.

Duty to Avoid Conflicts of Interest

A fiduciary must ***avoid*** situations where their personal interests conflict with those of the policyholder. If a conflict of interest arises, a fiduciary is typically required to disclose this conflict and, in many cases, recuse themselves from the decision-making process related to the conflict.

Duty to Act According to the Terms of the Fiduciary Agreement

Fiduciaries must adhere to the terms and conditions set forth in the agreement or legal instrument that established the fiduciary relationship. This includes following any specific instructions or guidelines stated in the contract.

Duty to Not Co-mingle Funds

Public adjusters must keep the beneficiary's funds and

property separate from their own. Commingling of funds can lead to conflicts of interest and mismanagement of assets.

Duty to Be Impartial

If a public adjuster serves multiple policyholders, they must treat all fairly and impartially. They should not favor one policyholder over another unless explicitly directed by the terms of the retention agreement.

RESOLVING CLAIMS DISPUTES AND CHALLENGES

Professional Dispute Handling

Handling claims disputes requires a balance of professionalism and fairness. This approach ensures all parties involved are heard and respected. It involves thoroughly assessing all aspects of loss, understanding and anticipating all viewpoints, carefully considering the policy language to craft arguments for coverage, and working towards a resolution that is equitable and satisfactory.

Advocacy With Integrity

Advocating for policyholders, while maintaining objectivity and integrity, is a delicate balance that requires skill, ethical judgment, and a deep understanding of insurance laws and policies. This involves standing up for the rights of the policyholder, while also considering the perspectives of the insurance carrier, to reach a fair outcome. Public adjusters should maintain as a reference *When Words Collide: Resolving Insurance Coverage and Claims Disputes* by Bill Wilson.

Alternative Dispute Resolution

In many cases, alternative dispute resolution methods, such as mediation or appraisal, can be more effective than traditional litigation. These methods often lead to quicker, more amicable resolutions, saving time and resources for all parties involved. They provide a platform for constructive dialogue and can often preserve relationships between policyholders and insurers. The rights and proper course between litigation and appraisal calls for application of facts to law. Giving advice to choose one or the other is the practice of law which public adjusters should not do.

UPHOLDING INTEGRITY AND TRUST

Applying Ethical Frameworks

Utilizing ethical frameworks is essential in making informed decisions. These frameworks provide a structured approach to evaluate the implications of various actions, ensuring decisions are made with a clear understanding of their ethical dimensions. This process involves considering that the obligations of a public adjuster apply to policyholders, insurance carriers, the insurance industry and the public adjusting profession. By applying these frameworks, public adjusters can better navigate often complex situations, ensuring their decisions align with ethical standards.

Considering Impact

Every decision made by a public insurance adjuster should be weighed for its potential impact on all involved parties. This holistic view is crucial for ensuring balanced and fair outcomes. It involves evaluating how decisions affect policyholders' well-being, the standing of insurance carriers, and the overall integrity of the industry. This comprehensive consideration helps in making choices that are not only legally sound but also ethically robust.

Seeking Guidance

Facing complex ethical dilemmas is not uncommon in the adjusting field. In such situations, seeking guidance from peers, mentors, industry experts, and attorneys can be invaluable. This collaborative approach allows adjusters to gain different perspectives and insights, enriching the decision-making process and making certain that laws and regulations are followed. It underscores the importance of not working in isolation but being part of a professional community that upholds ethical standards.

Conducting Honest Business

The foundation of trust in the public insurance adjusting sector is built on honesty, integrity, and transparency. These principles should guide all business practices. This approach not only builds trust with policyholders and insurance carriers but also enhances the credibility and reputation of the adjuster and the profession.

Accuracy and Truthfulness

Providing accurate and truthful information is a fundamental responsibility. It ensures policyholders and even insurance carriers are equipped with the necessary information to make informed decisions about submitted claims and settlement. This commitment to truthfulness based upon exacting information supporting the claimed loss is critical in maintaining the trust stakeholders place in public adjusters and the insurance process.

Avoiding Deception

It is imperative to steer clear of any misleading or deceptive practices. Such actions not only erode trust but can also have legal ramifications. They can significantly damage the public adjuster's reputation and the public's perception of the public adjusting industry. Maintaining honesty in all dealings reinforces the adjuster's commitment to ethical practices. "Half-truths" can be seen as misleading or deceptive.

RICH'S STORY

ETHICAL PRACTICES

As Rich's public adjusting business flourished, he found himself increasingly aware of the ethical challenges that permeated the industry. He witnessed firsthand how some adjusters and insurance professionals cut corners, inflated claims, or misrepresented facts to expedite settlements or increase payouts. These practices, while tempting for their potential short-term gains, deeply troubled Rich.

Rich understood the pressures that could lead to ethical compromises. The desire to win cases, satisfy clients, and grow his business was ever-present. However, he remained steadfast in his commitment to integrity, constantly checking himself and his team to ensure they operated within ethical boundaries.

One particularly challenging case tested Rich's resolve. A high-profile client hinted at the possibility of inflating a claim, suggesting it would be mutually beneficial. Rich faced a moment of truth – the potential financial gain was significant, but the cost to his integrity and professional license was immeasurable. Without hesitation, Rich declined, explaining to the client the importance of honest and accurate claim representation.

This unwavering commitment to ethics sometimes meant losing clients to less scrupulous competitors. However, Rich found that his reputation for honesty and fairness attracted a loyal clientele who valued trustworthiness above all else.

Rich implemented regular ethics training for his team, fostering a culture where ethical considerations were at the forefront of every decision. He encouraged open discussions about ethical dilemmas and celebrated instances where team members chose integrity over expediency.

Through it all, Rich remained true to his word, his license, and his fiduciary responsibility understanding that his ethical practice was not just about following rules, but about upholding the trust placed in him by his clients and the industry. This unwavering commitment to ethics became a cornerstone of his business, setting a standard that elevated not just his own practice, but the profession as a whole.

CHAPTER 15
SCALING AND FUTURE GROWTH

> If you want to go fast, go alone. If you want to go far, go together.
>
> AFRICAN PROVERB

STAYING nimble and proactive in identifying growth opportunities is paramount. It's not merely about maintaining pace with the market but anticipating its shifts and positioning your firm to capitalize on emerging trends and unmet needs. Let's embark on a journey through the strategic process of assessing market demand and trends to steer your firm toward sustainable expansion and success.

MARKET RESEARCH

Embarking on the quest for growth begins with comprehensive market research. Imagine yourself as a navigator charting unknown territories. Your map? The data you gather on market conditions, client needs, and competitor actions. Through surveys, industry reports, and direct feedback from clients, you can paint a detailed landscape of the current market, identifying both the challenges and the treasures hidden within. Use the skills we emphasized in Chapter 4.

NAVIGATE INDUSTRY TRENDS

Staying ahead requires more than just a keen eye on the present; it demands foresight. Like a lookout in the crow's nest, keep your gaze fixed on the horizon for emerging trends within the insurance industry. From regulatory changes to technological advancements and evolving client expectations, understanding these trends allows you to steer your firm towards opportunities before they become the new norms.

IDENTIFY MARKET GAPS

In the vast ocean of the public insurance market, there are still uncharted territories — gaps waiting to be filled by those bold enough to explore them. Whether it's a specific type of claim that's underserved or innovative client service approaches, identifying these gaps offers a pathway to diversification and growth. It's about finding your niche where you can not only compete but dominate. Here are some ideas:

- Hurricane Damage — Focus on claims from storm and wind damage in hurricane-prone areas.
- Flood Damage — Specialize in water-related damages, a common issue in many regions.
- Earthquake Damage — Handle claims related to seismic activities, crucial in earthquake-prone zones.
- Fire Damage — Specialize in residential and commercial fire claims.
- Mold Damage — Focus on claims arising from mold, which can be complex and contentious.

- Hail Damage — Specialize in the assessment of hail impact on properties, particularly in Midwest states.
- Windstorm Damage — Handle claims specifically for damages caused by non-hurricane-related winds.
- Theft and Vandalism — Specialize in claims arising from criminal activities.
- Tornado Damage — Focus on damage caused by tornadoes, common in certain areas of the country.
- Business Interruption — Specialize in claims involving lost income and extra expenses due to covered perils.
- Plumbing Leaks — Handle claims related to plumbing issues, including burst pipes.
- Electrical Damage — Focus on electrical malfunctions and their impacts on properties.
- Roof Damage — Specialize in roof integrity and related claims.
- Builders Risk Claims — Handle claims occurring during construction or building.
- Smoke Damage — Specialize in claims arising from smoke and soot, often a result of fires.
- Vehicle Impact — Handle claims where vehicles have caused property damage.
- Product Liability — Specialize in damages caused by defective products.
- Agricultural Losses — Focus on claims related to crop failures and livestock losses.
- Termite Infestation — Handle collapse damages caused by termites.
- Cyber Attacks — Specialize in losses due to cyber incidents affecting businesses.
- Snow and Ice Damage — Handle claims related to heavy snowfalls and ice damaging properties.

- Environmental Claims — Specialize in claims involving environmental pollutants and contamination.
- Marine and Cargo Claims — Specialize in losses related to marine and transport sectors.
- Aviation Claims — Focus on damages related to the aviation industry.
- Art and Antiques — Specialize in high-value personal property claims.
- Historical Property Damage — Focus on claims related to heritage and historical buildings.
- Loss of Use — Specialize in claims where properties become uninhabitable or unusable.
- Terrorism-Related Damage — Handle claims arising from acts of terrorism, requiring specific expertise and sensitivity.
- Urban vs Wildfire Claims--Specialty fire claims processing and issues occurring In a geographic location.

NEW HORIZONS: GEOGRAPHIC EXPANSION

Consider the world as your marketplace, with each region presenting unique opportunities for growth. Assessing the feasibility of expanding into new territories requires a careful analysis of market size, demand, and the competitive landscape. But remember, every new market comes with its own set of rules —local regulations, competition, and client needs must be meticulously evaluated to ensure a successful voyage.

EXPAND SERVICE OFFERINGS

The quest for expansion isn't just about where you go; it's also about what you offer. Identifying additional services that complement your core operations can open new revenue streams. From specialized claim services to consulting or claim-adjacent solutions, ensure these new offerings not only align with your expertise but also respond to clear market demands.

ASSESS RESOURCES AND CAPABILITIES

Before setting sail on your expansion journey, take stock of your vessel. Does your firm possess the necessary resources and capabilities to support this growth? Consider staffing, training, technology, and financial resources. Identifying gaps early allows you to chart a course to acquire or develop these capabilities, ensuring your expansion efforts are both effective and sustainable.

DATA ANALYTICS

In today's digital age, data analytics offers a powerful telescope to gaze into the market's depths, uncovering insights that traditional methods might miss. Leverage existing business analytics to identify patterns, preferences, and opportunities, providing a data-driven foundation for your expansion strategies.

ENGAGE INDUSTRY EXPERTS

Sometimes, the most direct path to unexplored markets is guided by those who have navigated similar journeys. Engaging with industry experts and consultants can illuminate opportunities and challenges you might not have considered, offering invaluable insights into niche areas or untapped markets.

WATCH COMPETITORS

Keep a watchful eye on your competitors as they, too, are navigating these waters. Their movements can reveal market trends, potential opportunities, or areas where you can differentiate your services. Understanding their strategies can provide strategic insights into your own path forward.

TEST PILOT PROGRAMS

Before committing to full-scale expansion, consider launching pilot programs. These initiatives allow you to test the market's response to your services in a new geographic area or service line, providing valuable feedback and insights with minimal risk. Based on the success of these pilots, you can refine your approach and confidently chart your course forward.

FOSTER LOCAL PARTNERSHIPS

In new territories, alliances can be your anchor. Local partnerships, whether with businesses or industry players, can offer insights and support, easing your entry into the market. These collaborations can amplify your firm's reach and effectiveness, providing a solid foundation for growth.

ADAPT TO LOCAL MARKET NEEDS

Each market has its own rhythm and demands. Be prepared to tailor your services to meet the specific needs of each new territory. This flexibility not only enhances your appeal to local clients but also demonstrates your commitment to providing personalized, client-centered services.

BUILD A SKILLED TEAM

The strength of your expansion lies in the capability of your team. Ensure you have the right crew by hiring talent with the necessary expertise or investing in training for your current team. A skilled and adaptable team is your greatest asset in navigating new markets and services.

This approach is elaborated in Chip Merlin's book, *Mavericks and Merlins,* where he discusses the importance of building teams that are not just skilled but are also capable of pioneering new initiatives and driving innovation in the field of public adjusting.

As emphasized in *Mavericks and Merlins,* the synergy within a team can significantly amplify its effectiveness. This is achieved through regular team-building activities, open communication channels, and a clear articulation of goals. Each team member's understanding of how their role fits into the larger company objectives is crucial for cohesive action and mutual support.

PILOT TESTING AND FEEDBACK

Just as in geographic expansion, pilot testing new services allows you to gather direct feedback and fine-tune your offerings. This iterative process ensures your services not only meet market needs but also uphold the quality and standards your clients expect.

In charting the course for expansion, the journey of a public insurance adjusting firm is one of constant exploration, adaptation, and growth. By thoroughly assessing market demand and trends, and strategically positioning your firm to seize new opportunities, you can navigate the competitive landscape with confidence. Remember, the goal of expansion is not merely to grow in size but to deepen your firm's impact, delivering unparalleled service and advocacy to a broader range of clients. With careful planning, a keen eye on the market, and a commitment to excellence, your firm can achieve new horizons of success and client satisfaction.

DEVELOP A GROWTH STRATEGY

Charting a course for growth requires more than ambition; it necessitates a strategic approach grounded in clear goals and a deep understanding of the market landscape. As we delve into the intricacies of setting clear goals and objectives for business expansion, it's essential to remember that the true north of any growth strategy should always align with enhancing service excellence and client advocacy.

ENVISION YOUR FIRM'S FUTURE

Imagine standing at the helm of your firm, peering into the horizon. What do you see? Defining a clear vision for your expansion is akin to setting your coordinates for the journey ahead. Whether it's broadening your reach into new markets, diversifying your service offerings, or solidifying your presence in existing domains, having a crystal-clear vision acts as your guiding star. It's about envisaging a future where your firm not only grows in scale but also in its capacity to make a meaningful impact on the lives of those you serve.

TRACK MEASURABLE OBJECTIVES

With your destination in sight, the next step is charting the course. This means breaking down your vision into tangible, measurable objectives. Think of these as the milestones on your journey – be it financial targets, client satisfaction benchmarks, or specific operational goals. These objectives are not just markers of progress; they are the means by which you navigate your firm's growth, allowing you to steer the course with precision and adapt to the changing tides of the market.

ALIGN WITH THE MISSION

In the pursuit of growth, it's crucial that your expansion efforts sail in harmony with your firm's mission. Growth for the sake of growth can lead you astray. Instead, every goal set, every strategy devised, should resonate with your core purpose – to serve your clients with unwavering dedication and integrity. This alignment ensures that as your firm expands, it does so not just in size, but in its commitment to excellence and ethical practice in the public insurance adjusting industry.

DRAFT THE EXPANSION BUSINESS PLAN

Your business plan is the navigator's log of your journey, detailing every aspect of your expansion strategy. From the financial forecasts to the operational blueprints, this document serves as the operational manual for your growth. It's where you address the 'how' of your journey, outlining the steps you'll take, the resources you'll need, and the challenges you might face. A comprehensive business plan not only guides your efforts but also communicates your vision to stakeholders, rallying them behind your quest for expansion.

FINANCIAL PLANNING

No voyage is possible without the necessary provisions. Assessing the financial landscape and securing the resources for your journey is paramount. This involves a thorough analysis of the costs involved, from operational expansions to marketing efforts, and exploring the avenues for funding these initiatives.

Whether through reinvestment, loans, or partnerships, a robust financial plan ensures that your expansion efforts are not just visionary but viable.

LEAD WITH FLEXIBILITY

The seas of market demand and industry trends are ever-changing. Incorporating flexibility into your goals allows your firm to navigate these waters adeptly, adjusting your sails as conditions dictate. This agility is crucial for seizing emergent opportunities and mitigating unforeseen challenges, ensuring that your growth efforts remain both responsive and resilient.

TEAM GOAL-SETTING

An expedition's success is as much about the crew as it is about the captain. Involving your team in the goal-setting process not only grounds your objectives in the reality of your firm's capabilities but also fosters a collective commitment to achieving them. When your team sees their input reflected in the firm's direction, it cultivates a sense of ownership and dedication that propels your firm forward.

EXPAND WITH PRECISION

As you embark on this journey of expansion, it's essential to move forward with a strategic mindset, guided by clear objectives and a steadfast commitment to your firm's mission. By carefully planning your route, securing the necessary resources, and fostering a culture of flexibility and collaboration, your firm can explore new horizons while remaining steadfast in its dedication to client advocacy and service excellence. Remember, the journey of growth is not just about reaching new destinations but about enriching the path you take with purpose, integrity, and an unwavering focus on the needs of those you serve.

IMPLEMENT GROWTH INITIATIVES

Building a strong, cohesive team is the cornerstone of any public insurance adjusting firm poised for growth. It's about more than just filling positions; it's about curating a collective of skilled, adaptable individuals who are deeply aligned with the company's mission and values. Let's explore the essential steps and strategies for assembling this powerhouse team and setting the stage for your firm's successful expansion.

IDENTIFY FUTURE TALENT NEEDS

Picture your firm as a growing organism, evolving and expanding in response to the environment. As you chart your course towards growth, the first step is a thorough assessment of the talent landscape within your firm. Which skills are crucial for navigating new markets? Do you need seasoned adjusters with specific geographic expertise, or tech-savvy professionals to leverage digital advancements in claim processing? This assessment lays the groundwork for a targeted recruitment strategy that brings onboard the right mix of talent to propel your firm forward.

RECRUITMENT, HIRING, AND TRAINING

Navigating the talent pool requires a keen eye for not only identifying individuals with the necessary technical skills but also those who embody the culture and values of your firm. The hiring process becomes a critical compass guiding you towards candidates who are not just qualified but are also a cultural fit. Once onboard, investing in comprehensive training programs is pivotal. These programs ensure that new hires are not just acquainted with the operational aspects of their roles but are fully integrated into the fabric of your firm, ready to contribute to its growth trajectory.

ENSURE CULTURAL AND VALUE ALIGNMENT

The true strength of your team lies in its alignment with the firm's foundational values. During the onboarding process, emphasize the core principles that define your firm—client advocacy, ethical practice, and a commitment to excellence. This cultural indoctrination ensures that every team member, regardless of their role, contributes to the firm's mission, fostering an environment of mutual respect, trust, and collaboration.

STRENGTHEN INFRASTRUCTURE AND OPERATIONS

As your firm embarks on this expansion journey, the operational framework must evolve to support the increasing demands. This may entail enhancing IT infrastructure, expanding office spaces, or optimizing internal processes for efficiency. Technology, particularly, plays a pivotal role. Investing in state-of-the-art claim management systems and automation tools not only streamlines workflow but also significantly boosts productivity, allowing your team to focus on delivering exceptional client service.

CHART MARKETING AND BRANDING EXPANSION

With the stage set for growth, developing a robust marketing strategy is crucial for capturing new markets and audiences. This strategy should not only spotlight your firm's unique value proposition but also resonate with the specific needs and expectations of your new target demographics. Building a strong brand identity, underpinned by your firm's commitment to quality and integrity, becomes your beacon, attracting clients and establishing your firm's presence in uncharted markets.

LEADERSHIP DEVELOPMENT AND ADAPTABILITY

Leadership development is the keel that keeps your ship steady through the tumultuous waters of expansion. By nurturing leaders within your ranks, you ensure that your team is equipped with visionaries who can navigate challenges, inspire innovation, and drive the firm towards its growth objectives. Encouraging continuous learning and adaptability ensures that your team remains agile, capable of adjusting to market shifts and embracing new opportunities with expertise and confidence.

CONTINUOUS IMPROVEMENT AND CLIENT FOCUS

As your firm grows, the commitment to excellence in service delivery must remain paramount. This involves not just maintaining high standards of client advocacy but also continuously seeking ways to enhance the client experience. Regular feedback mechanisms, client service model optimizations, and a relentless pursuit of operational excellence are key to ensuring that your firm not only meets but exceeds client expectations.

Building a strong team for a public insurance adjusting firm is akin to assembling a crew for a grand voyage. Each member plays a critical role, contributing their unique skills and perspectives towards the firm's collective success. By carefully assessing talent needs, fostering a culture of alignment and growth, and continuously striving for operational excellence, your firm sets sail towards a horizon filled with opportunities for expansion and success. Remember, the strength of your team is the wind in your sails, propelling your firm forward in its mission to serve clients with unparalleled dedication and expertise.

MANAGE RISKS AND ENSURE SUSTAINABILITY

Navigating the complexities of regulatory compliance and legal considerations is crucial for public insurance adjusting firms, especially in the face of expansion. See Chapter 2 for the strategies and practices essential for adapting to these vital aspects, ensuring your firm's growth is both sustainable and aligned with industry standards.

KEEP ABREAST OF REGULATORY TIDES

The landscape of regulations is ever-evolving, with each geographical area presenting its own set of rules and compliance requirements. Staying informed and agile is akin to charting a course through shifting sands. Regularly monitor legislative changes and industry standards, adjusting your practices to remain compliant. This proactive approach not only safeguards your firm against potential legal pitfalls but also positions you as a trusted and reliable entity in the eyes of your clients.

ENLIST LEGAL EXPERTISE

In the complex waters of insurance law, having seasoned legal professionals by your side is invaluable. These experts serve as navigators, offering guidance through the intricacies of compliance, contracts, and legal disputes. Their insights ensure that your expansion efforts are built on a solid legal foundation, mitigating risks and fostering a culture of integrity within your firm.

RISK MANAGEMENT

Effective risk management is the compass guiding your firm through potential storms. By identifying and assessing risks associated with expansion—be it operational, financial, or reputational — you can devise strategies to navigate these challenges. Implementing robust risk management practices not only protects your firm but also reassures your clients and stakeholders of your commitment to operational excellence.

STRATEGIC PARTNERSHIPS

The journey of expansion is best undertaken with allies. Forming strategic partnerships with businesses and stakeholders that complement your services can unlock new avenues for growth. These collaborations, whether with construction firms, legal advisors, or technology providers, enhance your service offerings and extend your reach. Mutual respect and shared goals are the anchors of these relationships, driving collective success and opening doors to innovative solutions.

MEASURE PROGRESS

Setting clear KPIs is essential for navigating the path of growth. These metrics serve as beacons, illuminating your firm's progress towards its objectives and enabling timely adjustments to your strategies. Whether it's financial performance, client satisfaction, or market penetration, regularly evaluating these indicators ensures your expansion efforts remain on course.

ETHICAL PRACTICES AND CLIENT ADVOCACY

At the heart of public insurance adjusting is a commitment to ethical practices and client advocacy. As your firm grows, reinforcing this commitment becomes even more critical. It's the beacon that guides your actions and decisions, ensuring that every step taken in pursuit of expansion is done with integrity and in the best interest of the clients you serve.

SUSTAINABILITY BEYOND BUSINESS

In today's world, the impact of your business extends beyond the financial bottom line. Adopting sustainable practices demonstrates your firm's awareness of its broader social and environmental responsibilities. Whether it's through eco-friendly office initiatives or community engagement, these practices not only contribute to a better world but also resonate with clients and employees who value corporate responsibility.

BUILD A FLEXIBLE BUSINESS MODEL

The ability to adapt and pivot in response to market changes is the hallmark of a resilient business. For public insurance adjusting firms, this means developing a business model that can withstand fluctuations in demand, regulatory changes, and other external pressures. Diversifying services, creating multiple revenue streams, and maintaining a flexible operational structure are strategies that underpin a resilient and sustainable business model.

NURTURE INDUSTRY CONNECTIONS

Fostering strong relationships within the insurance industry, including with carriers, other adjusting firms, and professional associations, is invaluable. These connections provide insights, opportunities for collaboration, and a supportive network that can bolster your firm's growth and reputation.

CONTINUOUS IMPROVEMENT

Adapting to regulatory and legal considerations is not a one-time task but an ongoing journey. It requires continuous vigilance, a willingness to learn and adapt, and a commitment to upholding the highest standards of professionalism and ethics. By embedding these principles into the fabric of your firm, you ensure not just compliance, but a foundation of trust and excellence that supports sustainable growth.

Navigating the regulatory and legal aspects of expansion is a critical aspect of building a successful, sustainable public insurance adjusting firm. By staying informed, engaging expert guidance, implementing robust risk management, and fostering strategic partnerships, your firm can confidently pursue growth opportunities while maintaining its commitment to ethical practices and client advocacy. Remember, the goal of navigating these complexities is not just to avoid obstacles but to strengthen the trust and reliability that are the cornerstones of your firm's reputation and success.

RICH'S STORY

SCALING AND FUTURE GROWTH

Rich's public adjusting firm had come a long way since its humble beginnings. With a solid foundation built on experience, success, and even valuable lessons from past failures, Rich felt ready to explore new horizons of growth. He recognized that scaling his business would not only allow him to help more policyholders but also provide better career opportunities for his dedicated team.

As he contemplated expansion, Rich approached the challenge with the same methodical mindset that had served him well in claims handling. He began by conducting thorough market research, identifying underserved areas and emerging needs in the industry. Rich also analyzed his firm's strengths and weaknesses, ensuring that any growth plans would leverage their expertise while addressing any shortcomings.

Rich knew that scaling wasn't just about increasing numbers; it was about maintaining and enhancing the quality of service that had become his hallmark. He invested in advanced training programs for his team, preparing them for larger and more complex cases. Simultaneously, he embraced the advanced features of ClaimWizard, leveraging its powerful tools to streamline operations and efficiently manage a growing caseload. This technological edge allowed Rich's team to handle more claims with greater accuracy and speed, while maintaining their high standards of service.

The decision to expand geographically was carefully considered. Rich opened a satellite office in a neighboring state, leveraging his reputation while adapting to new regulatory environments. This move not only broadened his client base but also provided exciting opportunities for team members eager for new challenges.

Throughout the growth process, Rich remained committed to his core values of integrity and client-centric service. He understood that scaling his business meant not just growing in size, but also in impact and influence within the industry.

As his company expanded, Rich found a renewed sense of purpose. The ability to help more policyholders, provide rewarding careers for his team, and increase profitability reinforced his belief that ethical, well-managed growth was the key to long-term success in the public adjusting field.

AFTERWORD

As you embark on your journey in the public insurance adjusting industry, remember, the landscape you're navigating is as complex as it is dynamic. With its intricate regulations and rapid technological advancements, your commitment to continuous learning and adaptation isn't just advantageous—it's imperative. Think of it as setting sail on open waters; to chart a successful course, you must be keenly aware of the changing currents and ready to adjust your sails as needed.

Make ongoing education your beacon. This journey of learning isn't a one-off endeavor but a continuous voyage. Seize every chance to deepen your expertise, from engaging in workshops and webinars to pursuing advanced courses. The deeper your knowledge well, the more effectively you can advocate for your clients, armed with the latest insights and information.

But your education extends beyond the classroom. Dive into industry forums and networks, exchanging ideas and challenges with peers. This vibrant community offers not just insights but real-world solutions and camaraderie. It's here, in the exchange of experiences with fellow professionals, that learning becomes truly transformative, equipping you with practical, battle-tested strategies.

Embrace perseverance as your guiding star. The path to success in this field is strewn with challenges and setbacks. Yet, each obstacle is a stepping stone, an opportunity for growth. Whether it's mastering complex claims, negotiating with tough insurance carriers, or adapting to new regulations, view each challenge as a puzzle to be solved, not a barrier to your progress.

Moreover, as you navigate your own journey, consider the value of guiding others. Mentorship enriches both mentor and mentee, forging a path for the next generation of adjusters. By sharing your knowledge and experiences, you not only aid others in their professional journeys but also contribute to a culture of excellence and continuous improvement in the public adjusting community.

In fostering a commitment to ongoing learning and demonstrating resilience in the face of industry challenges, you not only propel your own career forward but also raise the standard of the profession. This approach underscores the significance of expertise and integrity in public insurance adjusting, ensuring that you, and those who follow, are well-equipped to navigate the complexities of the insurance world.

HOW RICH IS DOING NOW

AS RICH REFLECTED on his journey in the public adjusting field, he couldn't help but marvel at how far he'd come. From the early days of uncertainty and learning to his current position as a respected industry leader, every step had been a lesson in perseverance, ethics, and adaptability.

Rich's firm had grown from a one-man operation to a thriving business with multiple offices, serving policyholders across several states. He took pride in the team he had built — dedicated professionals who shared his commitment to integrity and client advocacy. The advanced features of ClaimWizard had become an integral part of their operations, enabling them to handle an ever-growing caseload with efficiency and precision.

Looking back, Rich recognized that his success wasn't just measured in financial terms. It was evident in the lives he and his team had positively impacted, the complex claims they had successfully navigated, and the industry standards they had helped elevate. His reputation for ethical practices and unwavering commitment to policyholders' rights had become a benchmark in the field.

As he contemplated the future, Rich saw endless

possibilities. He envisioned expanding his firm's reach, possibly nationwide, while maintaining the personalized service that had been his hallmark. He dreamed of mentoring the next generation of public adjusters, passing on the wisdom he had gained through years of experience.

Rich's journey had taught him that true success in public adjusting came from a blend of knowledge, integrity, and genuine care for clients. He had found fulfillment not just in building a profitable business, but in making a meaningful difference in people's lives during their most challenging times.

As he looked forward to the next chapter of his career, Rich couldn't help but smile. He had achieved a level of success and satisfaction that he once thought impossible.

After all... don't you want to be "Rich?"

APPENDIX

LICENSING AND CERTIFICATION REQUIREMENTS FOR PUBLIC INSURANCE ADJUSTERS

Licensing requirements for public insurance adjusters vary significantly from state to state, reflecting the diverse legal and insurance landscapes across the United States. These requirements are put in place to ensure that adjusters possess the necessary knowledge, skills, and ethical grounding to effectively represent policyholders. Public adjusters must be aware that some states do not license public adjusting. A few states prohibit the practice of public adjusting. Other states may limit what a public adjuster may do on behalf of a policyholder regarding negotiation of a claim and the advice which may be given to a policyholder. No state allows a public adjuster to take actions or provide legal advice which is to practice law.

STATE-SPECIFIC REQUIREMENTS

Each state has its own set of requirements for licensing public insurance adjusters. These can include age, education, experience, and residency requirements. Some states may also require adjusters to pass a criminal background check.

APPLICATION PROCESS

The process typically involves submitting an application to the state insurance department, along with any required documentation and fees. The application process is designed to verify the adjuster's qualifications and readiness to serve the public.

UNDERSTAND THE QUALIFICATIONS, EXAMINATIONS, AND CONTINUING EDUCATION OBLIGATIONS

The path to becoming a licensed public insurance adjuster involves meeting specific qualifications, passing examinations, and fulfilling ongoing education requirements.

QUALIFICATIONS

Qualifications may include a minimum age, a high school diploma or equivalent, and sometimes a certain amount of experience in the insurance industry or a related field. Some states require sponsorship by an already licensed adjuster.

EXAMINATIONS

The licensing examination is a critical component of the process. It typically covers a wide range of topics, including insurance laws, policy types, claim handling procedures, and ethical standards. The exam ensures adjusters have a comprehensive understanding of their role and responsibilities.

CONTINUING EDUCATION

Once licensed, adjusters are often required to complete continuing education (CE) courses to maintain their license.

These courses keep adjusters up to date with the latest developments in insurance law, claim handling practices, and ethical standards. CE requirements vary by state but are crucial for adjusters to remain competent and compliant.

IDENTIFY THE REGULATORY BODIES RESPONSIBLE FOR OVERSEEING LICENSING AND COMPLIANCE

Each state has a regulatory body, typically known as the Department of Insurance (DOI), responsible for overseeing the licensing and regulation of public insurance adjusters. These bodies play a crucial role in maintaining the integrity and professionalism of the field.

Role of the DOI

The DOI is responsible for setting the standards for licensing, conducting examinations, and enforcing compliance with state insurance laws and regulations. They also handle complaints against adjusters and can impose disciplinary actions for violations.

Compliance and Enforcement

The DOI monitors the activities of licensed adjusters to ensure compliance with state laws and regulations. This includes reviewing adjuster conduct, auditing continuing education compliance, and investigating consumer complaints.

Resources and Support

In addition to regulation and enforcement, many DOIs provide resources and support to help public adjusters understand their responsibilities and stay compliant. This may include publishing bulletins, offering educational programs, and providing access to legal and regulatory updates.

Understanding and complying with licensing and certification requirements is fundamental for public insurance adjusters. These requirements, which vary by state, ensure adjusters are qualified, knowledgeable, and up to date with the latest industry standards and legal developments. The state Departments of Insurance play a pivotal role in setting these standards, conducting examinations, and ensuring ongoing compliance. By adhering to these requirements, public adjusters not only fulfill legal obligations but also demonstrate their commitment to professionalism and ethical conduct in their practice.

Navigating Insurance Laws and Regulations

Navigating the labyrinth of insurance laws and regulations is a critical aspect of a public insurance adjuster's role. These laws and regulations, which vary from state to state and sometimes at the federal level, govern how claims are handled, define the rights and responsibilities of both policyholders and insurance carriers, and set standards for claims assessment, negotiation, and settlement. This section explores these facets in detail, providing insight into the complexities of insurance law and its practical implications for public adjusters.

OBTAINING NECESSARY LICENSES AND CERTIFICATIONS

The process of obtaining the necessary licenses and certifications to become a public insurance adjuster is a multifaceted journey that involves thorough research, meeting educational and experience criteria, preparing for, and passing licensing examinations, and submitting detailed applications. This section provides an in-depth look at each of these steps.

Researching Licensing Requirements

Each state has its own set of licensing requirements for public insurance adjusters. It is imperative for aspiring adjusters to research these requirements thoroughly. This research should include understanding the scope of practice allowed under each license, any reciprocity between states, and specific state mandates regarding insurance adjusting.

Online resources, including state Department of Insurance

websites, are valuable for accessing up-to-date information on licensing requirements.

IDENTIFY NECESSARY DOCUMENTATION, FORMS, AND FEES

Licensing typically requires various forms of documentation, such as proof of identity, character, educational qualifications, and professional experience. Applicants must also be aware of the necessary forms to be filled out for the application process, which can often be sourced from the state's insurance department website.

Understanding the fee structure for application, examination, and license renewal is also crucial, as these fees can vary significantly between states.

MORAL FITNESS AND SURETY BONDS

The requirements for public adjusters in terms of moral fitness, criminal history, and surety bond obligations are essential components of the licensing process, designed to ensure the integrity and trustworthiness of professionals in this field. These requirements can vary by state, but there are common themes across jurisdictions:

◆ **Moral Fitness**

Moral fitness refers to the character and ethical standards expected of a public adjuster. This typically includes honesty, integrity, and professional conduct. Applicants may be required to provide character references or undergo an interview process to assess their moral fitness. Regulatory bodies often look for a history of ethical behavior, both in professional and personal capacities.

◆ **Felonies or Misdemeanors**

Most states require applicants to disclose any criminal history, including felonies and misdemeanors. The presence of a criminal record does not automatically disqualify an applicant, but certain types of offenses, particularly those involving fraud, dishonesty, or financial crimes, are likely to be scrutinized more closely. The recency and relevance of the criminal offense, as well as any patterns of illegal behavior, are typically considered. Rehabilitation efforts and character references can also play a role in the evaluation process. Some states have specific statutes or regulations outlining which offenses may disqualify an applicant from obtaining a public adjuster license.

◆ **Surety Bond Requirements**

Public adjusters are often required to obtain a surety bond before being granted a license. The surety bond acts as a financial guarantee that the adjuster will adhere to applicable laws and ethical standards in their practice. The amount of the surety bond required varies by state but typically ranges from $5,000 to $50,000. This bond protects consumers by providing a source of compensation in cases where the adjuster engages in fraudulent or unethical behavior.

To obtain a surety bond, the adjuster usually needs to pay a premium, which is a fraction of the bond amount. The premium amount can be influenced by the adjuster's credit score and professional history. These requirements are in place to protect policyholders and the integrity of the insurance adjusting process. By ensuring that public adjusters meet high standards of moral fitness, have a clean or suitable criminal record, and are backed by a surety bond, regulatory bodies aim to maintain trust and professionalism within the industry. It's important for aspiring public adjusters to understand and meet these requirements to successfully obtain and maintain their licenses.

SEEK GUIDANCE FROM REGULATORY AGENCIES OR INDUSTRY ASSOCIATIONS

Regulatory agencies are a primary source of authoritative information and can provide clarity on complex licensing requirements. Industry associations, such as NAPIA, offer limited resources and guidance for professionals entering the field. Most public adjuster organizations usually cater to those who are already licensed.

MEETING EDUCATIONAL AND EXPERIENCE CRITERIA

Understand Educational and Experience Prerequisites

Most states require a minimum level of education, such as a high-school diploma or equivalent, for licensing as a public insurance adjuster.

Some states may require or prefer a college degree, particularly in related fields, such as finance, law, or business.

Complete Required Courses, Training Programs, or Apprenticeships

Many states require specific pre-licensing courses or training programs that cover relevant laws, ethical standards, and technical aspects of insurance adjusting. Apprenticeships or mentorship programs under licensed adjusters can provide practical experience and insights into the profession. Those seeking apprentice or mentorship programs should seek public adjusting firms with great reputations and significant experience in the field.

Gain Relevant Experience in the Insurance Industry

Hands-on experience in the insurance industry, whether in claims processing, underwriting, or a related field, is often a prerequisite for licensure. This experience helps in understanding the practical aspects of insurance policies, claim handling, and client interactions.

Preparing for Licensing Examinations

- Develop a Study Plan and Gather Necessary Study Materials
- Set a Study Schedule
- Incorporate Different Learning Methods
- Assemble Essential Study Materials
- Online Resources and Study Guides
- Engage in Practice Exams and Mock Tests

Submitting Applications and Supporting Documents

- Assemble All Required Documentation
- Complete License Application Forms Accurately and Comprehensively
- Submit Applications Within Specified Timelines and Follow Submission Guidelines

ABOUT CHIP

WILLIAM "CHIP" MERLIN

In the ever-evolving landscape of property insurance law, few names resonate with as much authority and experience as Chip Merlin. President and founder of the Merlin Law Group, Chip Merlin has established himself not only as a preeminent advocate for policyholders but as a leading expert in the realm of property insurance and bad faith law. His comprehensive understanding and proactive approach in representing policyholders in disputes with insurance companies positions him as a pivotal figure for public adjusters seeking guidance and leadership in their profession.

Chip Merlin's journey in the legal field is built on a robust educational background and a profound commitment to justice. A proud alumnus of the University of Florida, he earned both his undergraduate and law degrees there.

Chip Merlin's career is marked by a series of achievements and roles that underscore his dedication to the policyholder community. As president of the Merlin Law Group, he leads a team of over 45 attorneys across the United States. This nationwide reach ensures that policyholders from every state have access to top-tier legal representation, particularly in disputes where insurance companies fail to act in good faith.

Chip Merlin's expertise is not confined to courtroom justice. He has closely worked with public adjusters for four decades, delivering his first speech to the National Association of Public Insurance Adjusters at its 1985 national convention. He helped co-found the Florida Association of Public Insurance Adjusters (FAPIA) in 1993. He has been at the forefront of educational initiatives, frequently lecturing and writing extensively on topics crucial to policyholders and public adjusters. His writings and seminars are not just informative; they are designed to empower and inspire action, offering new perspectives and strategies to handle complex insurance cases and promote the growth of public adjusters as a profession rather than a trade. He has published the Property Insurance Law Blog on a daily basis for nearly two decades.

Recognition of Chip Merlin's contributions comes from various prestigious organizations, attesting to his impact and leadership in the field. He has received a Lifetime Achievement Award from United Policyholders. He was designated as a Person of the Year by the National Association of Public Insurance Adjusters. He received a Lifetime Achievement Award from the Florida Association of Public Insurance Adjusters. Further, his tenure as President of the Windstorm Insurance Network and his receipt of the Eagle Talon Award from the Florida Justice Association highlight his contributions to legal excellence and policyholder rights.

Chip also helped organize the Professional Public Adjusters Association of New Jersey (PPAANJ) and the Rocky Mountain Association of Public Insurance Adjusters (RMAPIA.) He helped re-organize the Texas Association of Public Insurance Adjusters following Hurricane Ike. Understanding the critical role of public adjusters in the insurance claims process, Chip Merlin has dedicated significant efforts towards educating claims professionals. His aim is not just to inform but to elevate the practice of public adjusters, enhancing their ability to assist policyholders effectively. Through his teaching and published works, Chip Merlin provides public adjusters with the legal insights and tools necessary to navigate the complexities of insurance claims, ensuring they are well-equipped to advocate for the policyholder's best interests.

Chip Merlin's vision extends beyond individual cases. His goal is to position the Merlin Law Group as the best policyholder law firm in the United States. This ambition drives continuous improvement and innovation within the firm, ensuring that each client receives unparalleled service and representation. For public adjusters, this means having a reliable and authoritative ally in the legal realm, someone who not only understands the intricacies of insurance law but who can also anticipate and react to industry changes and challenges.

For public adjusters, Chip Merlin is more than an attorney; he is a mentor, educator, and advocate. His credentials and unwavering dedication to policyholder rights makes him an invaluable resource for public adjusters striving to excel in their profession. As public adjusters navigate their crucial role in helping policyholders achieve fair settlements, they can look to Chip Merlin not just for legal representation but for inspiration and guidance on how to advocate fiercely and effectively in a challenging industry.

facebook.com/MerlinLawGroup

instagram.com/MerlinLawGroup

ABOUT LYNETTE

LYNETTE YOUNG CMP/T, CCP, CBA

Lynette Young's career serving the public adjusting industry spans over 27 years, where she has worked with companies across five countries, providing a wealth of experience in business strategy and process design. Her unique skill set is underscored by her credentials as a ClaimWizard Mastery Program/Trainer (CMP/T), a Clockwork Certified Partner™ (CCP), and a Certified Business Advisor (CBA). This mix of experience and certification has allowed her to construct robust business infrastructures and develop operational workflows that drive success in public insurance adjusting.

As the co-founder of ClaimWizard, Lynette helped create a pioneering software platform designed to streamline public adjusting processes, making the entire process more efficient and accessible. Her innovative approach has revolutionized the way public adjusters manage their businesses, allowing them to focus on what truly matters: serving their clients. Lynette's deep understanding of the first party insurance claim business process and her unique ability to simplify complex concepts have made her a highly sought-after speaker and thought leader, frequently sharing her insights with professional audiences across the nation.

Beyond her technical acumen, Lynette has demonstrated exceptional skills in building strong client relationships and fostering an environment of collaboration and trust. She has consistently proven her ability to identify operational inefficiencies and rectify them, leveraging technology to optimize business practices. Her strategic insights are invaluable in today's fast-paced business landscape, where efficiency and clarity are crucial to success.

Lynette's guidance in deploying integrated systems for sustained business growth and scalability has equipped public adjusting companies to attract new clients and retain them by providing top-notch service and support. This holistic approach ensures that businesses can achieve enduring prosperity and expansion.

In collaboration with Chip Merlin, Lynette has authored a book that explores the complexities of public adjusting, providing readers with a comprehensive understanding of the industry. Through this work, she is determined to empower and enlighten professionals about the challenging but rewarding world of insurance claims, emphasizing the importance of collaboration with first-party insurance professionals. Lynette's ability to bridge the gap between complex business strategies and practical implementation makes her a respected leader in the public insurance adjusting space, inspiring others to embrace innovation and strive for excellence.

facebook.com/ClaimWizardSA
instagram.com/LynetteVYoung

www.ingramcontent.com/pod-product-compliance
Lightning Source LLC
LaVergne TN
LVHW010055220926
848484LV00005BA/1081